THE WRITTEN WORD IN PERFORMANCE

THE WRITTEN WORD IN PERFORMANCE

a history of drama and other literary forms
in Britain, Europe and the United States

by Paul Ranger

PUBLISHED BY
OBERON BOOKS
FOR THE LONDON ACADEMY OF
MUSIC AND DRAMATIC ART

First published in 2004 in association with LAMDA Ltd.
by Oberon Books Ltd.
(incorporating Absolute Classics)
521 Caledonian Road, London N7 9RH
Tel: 020 7607 3637/Fax: 020 7607 3629
oberon.books@btinternet.com
www.oberonbooks.com

ISBN: 1 84002 436 4

Cover design: Joe Ewart for Society

Printed in Great Britain by Antony Rowe Ltd, Chippenham.

CONTENTS

Other books by Paul Ranger

Experiments in Drama

The Lost Theatres of Winchester

A Masterguide to *She Stoops to Conquer*

A Masterguide to *The School for Scandal*

Terror and Pity Reign in Every Breast: Hanoverian Gothic Drama
on the London Stage, 1750–1820

Theatre in the Cotswolds
(in conjunction with Anthony Denning)

A Catalogue of Strolling Companies:
the ongoing theatre in Newbury

Performance

The Georgian Theatres of Hampshire

Meaning, Form and Performance

The Discussion: Second Edition
(in conjunction with Carol Schroder)

Under Two Managers: the everyday life of the Thornton
Barnett Theatre Company, 1785–1853

Bibliotheca Georgiana

Surveys on the gothic novel, the English garden from the
Middle Ages to the present, history of the British Theatre and
entries on eighteenth and nineteenth-century performers in
The New Oxford Dictionary of National Biography
The Readers' Guide to British History
The Continuum Encyclopaedia of British Literature

Sometime Editor of Speech & Drama

USING THIS BOOK

Introduction

This book is designed as a preparation for candidates studying to take Unit 1: Performance Theory (Viva Voce) of the Certificate in Speech and Drama: Performance Studies under the aegis of LAMDA Examinations. In this the candidate chooses one of a stipulated list of periods:

- Ancient Greece and Rome
- Elizabethan and Jacobean England
- Restoration England
- Georgian England
- Nineteenth-century Europe, including Britain
- Twentieth-century Europe, including Britain
- Twentieth-century America

The chapters in this book correspond to each of these periods and have the same format made up of:

- A survey of the drama and the theatres of the period
- A chronological table of the principal historical events of the period together with the plays and, where appropriate, other writings of the time
- A bibliography
- A list of discussion points
- References

Although this is the primary aim, the book also serves as a study guide to the history of British theatre and continental influences upon this as well as recent American drama.

Let us look at each of the sections that make up the chapters.

The survey

For easy reference this is divided into short sections each with a heading. From the survey you will learn of the principal playwrights of the period, and a couple of key texts of each writer's work are given. The survey should be used in conjunction with the bibliography. Sometimes a biography of a writer or performer is also suggested. At this juncture it should be pointed out that wide reading is essential to gain the background knowledge to deal successfully with this unit in the examination.

The chronology

This section lists important historical events for which the entries are indented. It is suggested that each event is followed up in an encyclopaedia. Get into the habit of making brief notes on events, plays and influences; for this purpose a ring binder is useful as the pages may be re-sorted as required.

The key plays of the period are also noted and may easily be recognised as there is an asterisk (*) immediately before the title. Sometimes researchers read a synopsis instead of the complete play, but as a drama is more than just a narrative, this can prove to be unsatisfactory. Specific poems and novels are also suggested occasionally and these too make an enjoyable read as well as giving a firm base to the study.

Bibliography

The bibliography looks somewhat formidable. However, it is a suggestion of the kind of books you should be reading. If you cannot get hold of those specified, then use similar works. Often more than one title is suggested to help with availability. Of course, it is not necessary to buy all of the books: library copies are adequate, especially with careful note taking. If you can obtain permission to use your nearest university library, this is most helpful; sometimes it is stipulated that non-registered students must read books in the library buildings. But you will need to have some reference works of your own. *The Oxford Companion to English Literature* is most valuable as are the related *Oxford Companions* to subjects such as theatre and painting. A paperback biographical dictionary can also be a helpful adjunct. It is recommended that candidates use this book in conjunction with Phyllis Hartnoll, *The Theatre: a Concise History*, revised edition 1995 published by Thames and Hudson; the illustrations are particularly useful.

Points for discussion

These are an indication of the kind of reflections that should be going through your head as you read and they form suggestions for discussion topics.

Notes and references

Notes and references usually relate to quotations in the text. This is the place to point out that a few brief quotations can be illuminating when speaking about a play and they may be most effectively used when learned by heart.

The last word

Try to think of your study as an enjoyable adventure. Use every means you can think of to advance it: theatre visits are most important when key plays are staged; visits to see historic theatre buildings are highly worthwhile; lectures given locally at bookshops, libraries and evening classes can be informative; a video or film version of a play script is better than nothing. Good luck!

GREEK AND ROMAN THEATRE

1. SURVEY

The beginnings

In Greek myth Dionysus was the god of wine and ecstasy. Representations of him varied. At simplest a column draped with a length of cloth was surmounted by a mask. In other places he was represented by a pretty youth reclining with grapes or a wine cup in his hand. In Roman times he was referred to as Bacchus and was shown as a florid, corpulent past-middle-aged fellow, still holding on to a symbol of wine. Devotion to Dionysus consisted of a unison hymn sung by a chorus of fifty men grouped around an altar in his honour. The hymn and the later movement were accompanied by a flute player who usually sat near the altar. From this kernel grew the Greek tragedy and the theatre, the place where this was performed.

The theatre at Epidaurus

The small state of Epidaurus is famed for its shrine to Asclepius, parts of which remain. The man-god was a medium for healing and the sick would visit the priests at the sanctuary where treatments were prescribed and given an opportunity to enjoy sleep therapy in the dormitory. Today, the chief glory of the place is the enormous Greek theatre, a part of the shrine, standing in a bowl of the landscape. Let us look at its principal sections. From wherever one stands, the *orchestra* is much in evidence, a large, paved circular area. Some social historians claim that this represents the threshing floor on which peasants beat the harvested wheat whilst they sang a hymn to Dionysus, separating the chaff, or unwanted outer parts of the ear from the usable inner parts. The earlier mentioned altar to Dionysus would have stood on a couple of steps at the circle's centre. Rows of stepped seats surrounded a little more than half the *orchestra* circle, an area known as the *theatron*, or the place from which the audience looked at the spectacle. The middle part of the front row was reserved for important officials such as the priest of Dionysus who sat on a carved stone throne, flanked by other priestly dignitaries. It has been estimated that the *theatron* at Epidaurus held up to 20,000 people.

Sitting in the *theatron*, the audience would look across the *orchestra* to the *proskenion* or raised, narrow stage that in turn was backed by the *skene*, a wooden one-storey building with a flat roof capable of supporting several actors. It seems likely that the Watchman in the *Agamemnon* would be placed up here and that the area also served for the *theologeion*, from which the gods intervene in Euripides' plays. At the front of this building either two or three doorways led on to the *skene* and these could be used for dramatic appearances such as the first of Oedipus from his palace in *Oedipus Rex* (*c*. 430 BC). Entrances by the performers was by way of a long, narrow *parados* situated between the end seats and the *proskenion*; actors could also make their way down several broad, shallow steps from the *skene* into the orchestra.

Although not strictly part of the structure of the theatre, there are two devices that should be mentioned. The first is the *ekkyklema*, a wheeled platform which may be drawn through doorways in the *skene* on to the front stage. On one of these would be arranged a tableau showing what had happened previously 'behind the scenes' such as the suicide of Jocasta in *Oedipus Rex*. Secondly, a device for flying characters was set up on top of the *skene* resembling a crane with an arm from which the actor was suspended. This was used when a god descended onto the *proskenion* and took over the action, a favourite device of Euripides.

Much material, such as costumes, scenic pieces, masks, wood and so on, were collected in the Greek theatre as in its modern counterpart and it is possible that this was stored inside the *skene* building; however, rooms for changing were separate from this, perhaps implying that the *skene* quickly became full of artefacts.

The chorus

We have already seen that the dithyrambic hymn to Dionysus was sung by a chorus prior to the seventh century BC; by the fifth century the chorus was used in the presentation of Greek tragedy. The three great tragic playwrights of these years were Sophocles, Aeschylus and Euripides. The first is reputed to have set the number of the chorus at fifteen – all men – and their tasks were through song, with flute accompaniment, speech and dance to comment on the progress of the action. Its members were 'disguised', that is to say masked, and they wore costumes appropriate to the characters they portrayed, such as the wretchedly ill people of Thebes in *Oedipus Rex*. This disguise was a religious requirement. The leader of the chorus was known as the *coryphaeus*. The normal entry point for the chorus was along the passage way to the right of the audience in a quadrangular form, three abreast. Once in the orchestra, there they stayed with the leader in the row nearest the audience.

The actors

In the earliest days of tragedy there was only one actor, the poet himself, but Aeschylus increased the number to two and Sophocles to three; this was the number at which Greek tragedy became set. As with the chorus, men (not boys, as in Shakespeare's day) played the women's roles. Only the leading performer was said to 'act' the play, his two fellow players gave a more restrained reading. These three actors could, of course, between them play more than three characters and it is instructive to take the roles in a tragedy and calculate how the doubling, and more, took place. One has to remember that silent extras were permitted.

The disguise: costumes and masks

An actor is someone who disguises himself and in the Greek theatre costume, mask and properties were the means of achieving this disguise. The original form of facial disguise used for dramatic performances was to treat the face with a white substance such as white lead then cover it with a red oxide of mercury or wine lees and finally the mask of untreated linen would be put on. A generation later masks were made of clay or stiffened linen, cork or wood. The fragility of these materials means that all we have of the mask designs are stone copies from statues. In the course of the play the main actor's face might be grossly changed; after Oedipus has gouged out his eyes the sockets stream with blood which runs down his cheeks so that a different mask is required. A feature of many masks is the huge, trumpet-shaped mouth, always wide open allowing sound to escape without impediment. The immensity of the theatre sometimes dictated that the mask should be exaggerated in size so that all spectators may easily see the character. Gradually the faces became set in traditional expressions, so that by the time of Julius Pollux, a social historian of the second century AD, the different roles are distinguished by the colour and style of the hair and the cut of a man's beard. Pollux lists 28 different patterns for masks.

The remaining part of the actor's costume was designed to integrate with the mask. The tragic actor's dress was luxurious in its texture and quantity of material, consisting of a long tunic reaching to the ankles over which a thick cloak was hung. In some plays Dionysus appears wearing tall hunting boots (*cothurni*) with brightly coloured thick soles.

Actors appearing in historical dramas tended to wear costumes contemporary with their time; sometimes this would be more colourful or extravagant. Emblems helped to identify characters; thus Apollo might hold his bow, Heracles would have a club and a lion skin, kings their sceptres, heralds their wreaths and the warrior would hold aloft his sword.

So much for the actor; what did the chorus wear? Naturally, masks and costumes would suit the principal factor of the group: thus old men would each carry a staff, wearing a three-quarter length tunic, and their disguise would be completed with a mask to which a beard was fixed. Women in mourning would be dressed in black tunics and their hair would be cut short to denote their sorrow; the Bacchae would wear their fawnskins and carry ivy-covered wands; the Furies, or Eumenides, would appear with snakes in their hair to match the description of the Pythian priestess at the beginning of the *Eumenides* (458 BC). Always their costumes emphasised that they were an integrated group.

The choral odes

We have noted that the chorus is present to speak, sing and dance and that the leader of the chorus engages one of the actors in conversation. Now we ought to be more precise, and to clarify we shall use one of the choric odes in *Oedipus Rex*; the translation by H D F Kitto suits our purpose.[1] In this play the chorus consists of Theban citizens. The play is divided into seven episodes, each of which terminates with a choric ode spoken, naturally, by the chorus. At the end of the first episode the group of fifteen Theban citizens (this number includes the chorus leader) enters the orchestra and takes up their position. Much of the first ode is spoken to a variety of gods whom it is hoped will heal the sickness that has visited Thebes. It is helpful to know that statues or paintings of gods decorated the front of the *skene* building; these are the 'shrines' addressed in the ode. Seven of the chorus members speak *Strophe* 1; it is probable that the other half of the chorus dance to the dactylic rhythm of their speaking. This *strophe* consists of ten lines. At the end of it the roles are reversed so that those who formerly spoke are now free to dance; this is known as the *Antistrophe* and is a mirror image of the *Strophe*. *Strophe* and *Antistrophe* 2 and 3 are then performed in the same fashion.

In triadic forms of the ode a verse known as the *epode* (meaning 'that which comes after') is sung either after each *strophe* and *antistrophe* or at the end of the ode. The epode need not mirror the pattern and metre of the *strophe* and *antistrophe*, thus giving a feeling of freedom and variety to the ode. In Kitto's translation of *Oedipus Rex* none of the odes is given an epode.

You need to know classical Greek if you are to understand the meaning of the terms referring to metre and, as few people have this knowledge, reference to them has been omitted. It is possible to feel the metre within you as you speak the words, especially in a translation such as Professor Kitto has given, as he is consciously bringing into it the various stress patterns of the original. However, if you wish to begin to study this topic, a clear entry is given in the *Oxford Concise Companion to Classical Literature* under the term 'metre'.[2]

The City Dionysia

In the fifth century BC at the end of March each year a festival was held in Athens known as the City Dionysia. A large theatre dedicated to the god nestled into one facet of the Acropolis that was built on the plateau of a steep-sided hill. Less of the theatre remains than at Epidaurus and the principal defect is that the farther end of the *orchestra* has been covered by the *proskenion* and only the lower rows of the *theatron* remain. The festival was under the management of the *Archon* (a figure who in some ways corresponded to an English mayor); the choice of the plays to present at the festival was in his hands, although all of the plays were judged on a competitive basis by the *kritai* from which our modern word 'critic' is taken. Four days (three during the Peloponnesian War) were devoted to the festival and on each day three tragedies, often related, were performed, the first beginning early in the morning and the third not finishing until late afternoon, after which a comedy brought the evening to a close. During the spread of the festival seventeen thousand people sat in the theatre; it was a matter of a citizen's duty to attend and financial help was awarded to the aged and indigent.

At its conclusion each of the ten judges of the festival cast a vote, recording his considered order of preference on a tablet placed in an urn. The names of the victorious poet and the *choregos* were announced and the *Archon* crowned them with a wreath of ivy. There were of course other ceremonies too, many of them religious, at least in origin and relating to Dionysus. A fuller account of the Dionysia is given in Baldry (see section 3).

Plays and playwrights

Why did an Athenian go to the theatre to watch a series of tragedies? There was a belief that to see a heroic character, a man of greater stature and status than the citizen members

of the audience, endure a reversal of fortune (riches to rags)
had a cathartic, or cleansing, effect on those watching the
play. This is a characteristic we shall find in each of the
tragedies mentioned. And the consequence was that each
person left the auditorium purged to some degree.

Aeschylus: *The Oresteia*

The earliest of the chosen playwrights is Aeschylus whose
complete trilogy *The Oresteia* was first performed in
458 BC or thereabouts. One gains the impression that one
is watching a fragment of the history of a dynasty, the
mythical family of Atreus. In the first play we learn a little
of the staging as the Watchman is looking out across the sea,
waiting for the return of the ruler Agamemnon; on the stage
he is raised up on the roof of the *skene*, an impressive, solo
figure at the start of a day of theatre. The doorway to the
skene plays an important part in *Agamemnon,* for the ruler,
on his return to Argos, prepares to make his way into the
palace. His entry along the *parados* in his chariot
accompanied by plunder as well as by his mistress,
Cassandra the sage, presages this importance but the purple
silk carpet leading into the royal house suggests that the
entrance is even more important. Almost everyone in the
theatron is in a position to see the carpet and most would
have known that rulers do not walk on silk carpets; that
honour is reserved for gods. Whilst still in the chariot
Agamemnon prays:

> Give me the tributes of a man
> And not a god, a little earth to walk on,
> Not this gorgeous work.[3]

However, Agamemnon is so overweening in his *hubris* or
pride that, encouraged by the welcome of Clytemnestra his
wife, he strides over the precious material, after first

removing his shoes. In this entry one sees that there is a curse on the house of Atreus. This is one example of the importance given by Greek playwrights to the disposition of the acting area and, fundamentally, what the various elements represent.

A further moment of visual strength is the revelation to the audience of the corpses of Agamemnon and of his concubine, Cassandra, murdered by Clytemnestra. These were presumably arranged on the *ekkyklema*, with Agamemnon in the silver salver, and drawn through the palace doors on to the *proskenion* by slaves; there is also the possibility that the bodies were raised through the roof of the skene and equally effectively displayed there.

As well as the visual pictures built up on the proscenium by the *choragus* or director of the play, there are the themes given to the actors by the playwright and in production these two elements become intertwined. The purple for the carpet about which I have written was obtained by crushing a small sea-beetle, the cochineal, and staining the material with it. This lends itself to further imagistic uses: the net in which the beetles are fished is referred to when the body of Agamemnon is revealed. Although one is in some doubt whether this is a figure of speech or an implied stage direction that a similar net is entangled around the corpse of the king. Clytemnestra says:

> He had no way to flee or fight his destiny –
> Our never-ending, all-embracing net, I cast it
> Wide for the royal haul, I coil him round and round
> In the wealth, the robes of doom, and then I strike him
> Once, twice...

Several lines later Aegisthus, the lover of Clytemnestra, takes up the net image but this time figuratively: '...now I see this monster in the nets of Justice'. It is Cassandra in her first set of short speeches who draws our attention to the blood infestation of the house of Atreus:

> ...the house that hates god,
> an echoing womb of guilt, kinsmen
> torturing kinsmen, severed heads,
> slaughterhouse of heroes, soil streaming blood...

But very quickly the seer gets down to tangible realities rather than figures of speech when she returns to the production by crushing of the crimson dye:

> Oh no, what horror, what new plot,
> new agony this? –
> it's growing, massing, deep in the house,
> a plot, a monstrous – thing
> to crush the loved ones, no,
> there is no cure, and rescue's far away...

We need to be aware that themes, icons, the stage geography, the ideas of the Grecian family dynasty are all part of the production and all have to be incorporated in telling the story.

The audience had to wait until the third play before it met the Eumenides (they give their name to the title), the strangest of the roles in the trilogy. Ironically they were known as 'the kindly ones' but in reality they were vengeful, pursuing females – the Pythian priestess at the start of the play describes them in emotive detail – who hunt down Orestes. His crime is that at the instigation of Apollo he has killed his mother, to avenge the death of his father Agamemnon. He has been pursued over the Hellenic world. The body of the play takes the form of a trial organised by the goddess Athena in which ten of the citizens of Athens as judges weigh up the case against Orestes. The method of indicating whether they feel Orestes is guilty or not is to place a ballot stone in an urn, an act which mirrors the method of the adjudicators at the festival: thus mythic past and present coalesce. It is noteworthy that when T S Eliot wrote *The Family Reunion* (1939) he used the figures of the Eumenides to hound down the hero, Harry, as he made his way back to Wishwood House, where they appear a couple of times in the embrasure of the drawing-room window.

Instead of ending on a note of quiet resolution, this trilogy works towards a grand concluding procession led by Pallas Athene and including the Eumenides, the judges, 'sacrificial victims, flaming torches, red robes and female attendants'.[4] It is both a civic and religious procession, illustrating admirably the intertwining of the two as an important part of Athenian life.

The shape of this play introduces us to the 'suppliant plot pattern', in which a suppliant (Orestes in this case) is pursued by vicious revengers (the Eumenides) and is rescued by a pious city (Athens): the pursuers are dismissed from the stage and a dramatic form of rejoicing (here a procession, in spite of the fact that Orestes has already left for Argos) takes place.

Sophocles: *Three Theban Plays*

As a boy Sophocles danced and led singing in the theatre where his beauty was admired. He first won the Great Dionysia in 468 BC at which he gained supremacy over Aeschylus. It was claimed that he wrote over 130 plays and won 24 dramatic competitions with his tetralogies. Aristotle tells us that he was an innovator: Sophocles wrote the part for a third actor in his tragedies and he increased the size of the chorus from a dozen to fifteen. It was Aristotle's opinion that the playwright's characters were 'like ourselves, only nobler' and Sophocles commented on the remark saying he depicted people as they ought to be. The heroes and heroines of his plays find themselves in circumstances in which they must act, even though this induces tragic consequences: but it is in battling with these circumstances that they reveal their heroic quality. Whereas Aeschylus wrote about the development of a family or a community and narrated this over three plays, Sophocles tended to make each tragedy complete in itself: it is the location in Thebes which holds the plays together.

If we take *Oedipus Rex* (sometimes translated *Oedipus the King*) as a sample of the three plays, one of the first impressions on looking at the text is that it is subdivided into Episodes, something from which *The Oresteia* was free. A preface begins the piece, taking place outside the royal palace at Thebes. With economy Sophocles tells the audience that a sickness has come to the city; a priest begs Oedipus for his help. The first episode is marked by the entry of a chorus of citizens awaiting the return of messengers sent to the Delphic oracle: in a time of peace why is there this dismay and illness? We hear glancingly of the death of King Laius, at a place where three roads meet. A blind seer, Teiresias, introduces the theme of blindness running through the play: the seer has no physical sight and Oedipus, sighted, is blind to his personal family history. As do most other seers Teiresias speaks in riddles: even the stick he carries resembles a measuring rod and we discover that Oedipus became King of Thebes because he solved the riddle of the sphinx. Each episode ends in the same manner with an ode which also prepares the audience for the next episode. Little progress is made when Oedipus speaks with Creon, the brother of his wife, Queen Jocasta. At this point it is important to remember that the plot is not a new mystery story confronting the audience but an ancient and well-known myth, the discovery by Oedipus of the reason for the pestilence in Thebes: the interest lies not so much in a mystery as in the way in which the plot is pieced together by Oedipus. From this point Oedipus meets a number of people – one discovery and one person per episode – and from them he learns that the shepherd he had accepted as his father was not so; he himself turns out to be the child of Laius whom he realises he slew at the three point cross-roads. He also learns that his mother is Queen Jocasta, whom he has since married, thus bringing incest to the house, or dynasty, of Laius. This is the moment of truth for Oedipus:

> ...I who am proved accursed in my conception,
> And in my marriage, and in him I slew.

Such a moment is known as the *anagnorisis* or flash of recognition. Aristotle in *The Poetics* comments on this moment in the tragedy:

> As the word indicates, a recognition is a change from ignorance to knowledge, and it leads either to love or to hatred between persons destined for good or ill fortune. The most effective form of discovery is that which is accompanied by a reversal, like the one in Oedipus...for a recognition of this kind in combination with a reversal will carry with it either pity or fear, and it is actions such as these that, according to my definition, tragedy represents...[5]

In order to create a unity of action any violence is usually narrated by a messenger rather than presented on the stage as in a Jacobean tragedy. Earlier the truth had become evident to Jocasta and she hung herself. The audience learnt of this by the employment of a servant who related the narrative. However, after the *anagnorisis* the palace doors open and Oedipus, wearing a specially constructed mask, slowly makes his way to the *proskenion*, blood streaming from his empty eye sockets: he has blinded himself to atone for the murder and the incest. The play ends with a long farewell from Oedipus to the city of Thebes and to his children: he is on his way to the mountain Cithaeron where he was first found as an abandoned baby, his feet swollen from being staked together, the literal meaning of 'Oedipus'. Unfortunately, the concluding utterance of the chorus has become lost.

The other two plays printed in this collection are *Oedipus at Colonus* (401 BC) a lead up to the death of Oedipus, blind and rejected and the *Antigone* (441 BC), possibly known now through Jean Anouilh's version (1944) which he wrote during the occupation of France in the second world war and made use of in the text.

Euripides: *The Bacchae*

Many stories are told about Euripides, most of them apocryphal, but we do know he was of a solitary disposition, partly because he had a poor image of himself, and was barely interested in politics. He was associated with the sophists, independent tutors who travelled from one cultural centre to another, giving lectures of an advanced academic standard. Towards the end of his life he moved from Athens to the court of Archelaus, King of Macedon, and died ripped to pieces by the king's dogs.

The chorus of *The Bacchae* (pre 406 BC) are the women who celebrate the new religion of the rites of Dionysus – who is also known as Bacchus – at a festival on Mount Cithaeron: the worship of Dionysus induced a state of ecstasy and was a far cry from the established rational expression of religion King Pentheus was upholding. So untypically the chorus of Bacchantes plays a highly active role in the drama. In the play Pentheus imprisons Dionysus after he has driven his suppliants on Cithaeron mad with desire. They hunt goats and cattle and tear them in pieces in fits of Bacchic madness. Possibly believing that the prey they have caught is imbued with the spirit of Dionysus, the women too are similarly possessed through the eating of the wild animals. The god induces Pentheus to disguise himself as a woman so that he may see the female rites on the mountain; he is discovered and Agavë, his mother, not recognising her son, decapitates him and mounts his head on the end of a *thyrsus* or pole as a hunting trophy. The other women tear him to pieces. Agavë bears the head of Pentheus to Thebes but on recovery from the ecstasy she discovers she has killed her son. The family are banished from the city.

The play is full of intriguing incidents as far as the plot and the stagecraft are concerned. One such is the earthquake which destroys the palace of Pentheus; how was this achieved as the solidly built *skene* represented the Theban palace? The singing of Dionysus, the sign of his presence with the suppliants, drives the women to a leaping frenzy and the whole effect of lightning, fires, earth tremors are entirely reliant on the choreography performed by them. One interpretation would be that the activity occurs only in the minds of the Bacchantes. Eventually the women fling themselves on the *proskenion* waiting for the arrival of Dionysus on the roof of the *skene*, only to find that the 'holy man' walks casually through the palace door, a parallel demonstration in movement of the unusually casual speech Euripides employs in the tragedy.

Aristophanes' comedies

How strange it is that so intense and sacrificial a tragedy as *The Bacchae* should provide the inspiration for Aristophanes' light hearted *Thesmophoriazusae* (411 BC): an elderly relative of Euripides attends this women's festival disguised as one of them; the ensuing adventures form the body of the play. Innovation was the butt for Aristophanes' satire: *The Birds* (414 BC) presents the impossibility of creating a new and harmonious state, even were it cloud-cuckoo-land and built by the freely flying birds; *The Frogs* (405 BC) queries the duties of a poet after the deaths of the fifth-century tragic triumvirate; *The Clouds* (423 BC) ridicules the sophists, using Socrates as their figurehead; *Lysistrata* (411 BC) is a moral protest against war in which the women of Athens refuse their husbands sexual relations and gain possession of the Acropolis and the state's finances. Eleven comedies survive, so there is an opportunity to extend the reading.

The Roman theatre

From such buildings as the theatre at Sabratha in North Africa and the Herod Atticus Theatre on the slopes of the Athens Acropolis we may judge the architectural changes that were made to the theatres built by the Romans, a contrast to the open spaciousness of the Greek theatre.[6] By AD 200 the chorus had disappeared from the drama leaving no need for the *orchestra*, although a semicircular space was usually provided. A raised stage of some depth was used by the actors backed by an elaborate *frons scaenae* sometimes three storeys high. Instead of the *parados* of the Greek theatre a rectangular doorway was provided at each side of the stage. The whole stage could be screened from view by a large curtain, the *aulaeum* which, instead of being raised, was dropped into a channel in the floor. Some of the Roman theatres were equipped with awnings over the audience to protect people from inclement weather. Around the perimeter of the complex ran a high masonry wall.

Three Roman playwrights should be mentioned: Menander, Plautus and Terence. Only one play by Menander has been pieced together from extant fragments, whilst his other writings are mere scraps. However, before many of these were found his sentiments were known by collections of epigrams, including a quotation which St Paul used in his first letter to the Corinthians: 'Evil communications corrupt good manners.' Some of the pithy remarks are ironic and acerbic such as the words spoken to an old man: 'Whom the gods love, die young.'

From the time of Shakespeare audiences have enjoyed certain scenarios which belong to the world of fiction rather than the events of daily life and many can be traced to Menander's plots. There is the plight of the abandoned child, the recognition of the long-lost youth from trinkets he carries, seductions of maidens of quality in the darkness of a night-time festival, and so on. We find too in the fragments often-repeated characters, the stock of English pantomime: there is the bragging soldier, the angry father and the kindly prostitute.

Twenty of the plays of Plautus have survived based on original Greek comedies: the episodes, in the hands of Plautus' are stock situations, brief and to the point, employing stock motifs such as the slave in a hurry, jokes and word play including puns and coarse badinage. Song and recitative feature in his plays at the expense of dialogue. *Menaechmi*, the plot of which is based on twin characters whose identity becomes mistaken, provided the basic idea for Shakespeare's *The Comedy of Errors* (1594 AD); but this gains from the employment of two pairs of twins.

Terence wrote six plays, some of which are adaptations of Menander's plots. However, Terence is a more subtle writer: caricature gives way to portraiture, conversations are natural without the lyric passages, background information is inserted into the dialogue rather than conveying tracts of information in a prologue. His writings have been presented in Europe in more recent times: the tenth-century Abbess Hroswitha in Saxony encouraged her Benedictine sisters to read him and in the sixteenth century the boys of St Paul's School gave performances of *Phormio* (*c.* 161 AD) from which the well-known phrase 'Fortune favours the brave' is filleted.

2. SELECTED AUTHORS, PLAYWRIGHTS AND WORKS OF THE CLASSICAL PERIOD

Note: Titles of plays are preceded by an asterisk. All dates given are BC.

c. 530: Beginnings of Attic Tragedy

490: First Persian invasion of Greece and the Battle of Marathon

480: Second Persian invasion of Greece

478–29: Domination of the Aegean by Athens

c. 460: *Prometheus Bound by Aeschylus [?]

458:    *The Oresteia by Aeschylus

c. 450–29: Periclean Age in Athens

441:    *Antigone by Sophocles

438:    *Alcestis by Euripides

431:    *Medea by Euripides

431–04: Peloponnesian War between Athens and Sparta

c. 430: *Oedipus Rex by Sophocles

423:    *The Clouds by Aristophanes

415:    *The Trojan Women by Euripides

411:    *Thesmophoriazusae by Aristophanes

c. 410: *Electra by Sophocles

405:    *The Bacchae by Euripides

405:    *The Frogs by Aristophanes

c. 405: *Oedipus at Colonus by Sophocles

404: Athens surrenders to Sparta

204:    *Miles Gloriosus by Plautus

?:   *Menaechmi by Plautus

?:   *Aulularia by Plautus

166:    *Andria by Terence

161:    *Eunuchus by Terence

3. BIBLIOGRAPHY

General works

Arnott, Peter, *An Introduction to the Greek Theatre*. London: Macmillan, 1959.

Baldry, H C, *The Greek Tragic Theatre*. London: Chatto and Windus, 1978.

Classical Literary Criticism, translated by Penelope Murray. Harmondsworth: Penguin Books, 1965.

Green, J R, *Theatre in Ancient Greek Society*. London: Routledge, 1994.

Grimal, Pierre, *Penguin Dictionary of Classical Mythology*. Harmondsworth: Penguin Books, 1991.

Hourmouziades, N C, *Production and Imagination in Euripides*. Athens: Hellenike anthropistike,1965.

Kott, Jan, *The Eating of the Gods: An Interpretation of Greek Tragedy*. New York: Random House,1973.

Lattimore, R, *The Poetry of Greek Tragedy*. Baltimore: Johns Hopkins University, 1958.

Lattimore, R, *Story Patterns in Greek Tragedy*. London: Athlone Press, 1964.

Pickard-Cambridge, A W, *The Dramatic Festivals of Athens*. Oxford: Clarendon Press,1968.

Simon, Erika, *The Ancient Theatre*, translated by C E Vafopoulou-Richardson. London: Methuen and Co Ltd, 1982.

Swaddling, Judith, *The Greek Theatre*. London: The British Museum, 1977.

Taplin, Oliver, *Greek Tragedy in Action*. London: Routledge, 1985.

Webster, T B L, *Greek Theatre Production*. London: Methuen, 1956, 2nd edition, 1970.

Illustrations

The following books are exceptionally well illustrated:

Bieber, M, *The History of the Greek and Roman Theatre*. Princeton: Princeton University Press, 1961.

Trendall, A D and T B L Webster, *Illustrations of Greek Drama*. London: Phaidon, 1971.

Playwrights and plays: Greek

Aeschylus

Aeschylus, *The Oresteia*, translated by Robert Fagles. Harmondsworth: Penguin Books, 1977.

Cornford, F M, 'Notes on *Oresteia*' in *Classical Review*, 53 (1939), 162–5.

Murray, G G A, *Aeschylus: The Creator of Tragedy*. London: Oxford University Press, 1962.

Rosenmeyer, Thomas G, *The Masks of Tragedy: Essays on Six Greek Dramas*. Austin, Texas: University of Texas Press, 1963.

Taplin, Oliver, *The Stagecraft of Aeschylus*. Oxford: Clarendon Press, 1977.

Winnington-Ingram, R P, 'Role of Apollo in the *Oresteia*' in *Classical Review*, 47 (1933), 97–104.

Aristophanes

Aristophanes, *The Birds and other Plays*, translated by Stephen Halliwell. Oxford: Oxford University Press, 1998.

Aristophanes, *The Frogs and Other Plays*, translated by David Barrett. Harmondsworth: Penguin Classics, 1964.

Demand, Nancy, 'The Identity of *The Frogs*', in *Classical Philology*, 65 (1970), 83–8.

Wycherley, R E, 'The Birds' in Classical Quarterly, 31 (1937), 22–31.

Euripides

Barlow, S, The Imagery of Euripides. Bristol: Bristol Classical Press, 1986.

Diller, H, 'Euripides final phase: The Bacchae' in Oxford Readings in Greek Tragedy, ed E Segal. Oxford: Oxford University Press, 1983.

Euripides, The Bacchae and other plays, translated by James Morwood. Oxford: Oxford University Press, 1999.

Grube, G M A, The Drama of Euripides. London: Methuen, 1941.

Murray, G G A, Euripides and his Age. London: Oxford University Press: 2nd edition, 1946.

Sophocles

Bowra, C M, Sophoclean Tragedy. London: Oxford University Press, 1965.

Clay, J H, 'The Antigone of Sophocles: a Production Concept' in Drama Survey, 3 (1964), 490–9.

Paolucci, A, 'The Oracles are Dumb or Cheat. A Study of the Meaning of Oedipus Rex' in Classical Journal, 58 (1963), 241–7.

Sophocles, Three Tragedies, translated by H D F Kitto. London: Oxford Paperbacks, 1962.

Vellacott, P H, 'The Chorus in Oedipus Tyrannus', in Greece and Rome, 14 (1967), 109–24.

Webster, T B L, An Introduction to Sophocles. London: Oxford University Press, 2nd edition, 1969.

Wilkins, John and Matthew Macleod, Sophocles, Antigone and Oedipus the King: A Companion to the Penguin Translation. Bristol: Bristol Classical Press, 1987.

Playwrights and plays: Roman

Plautus

Anderson, William Scovil, *Plautus Roman Comedy*. Toronto: University of Toronto Press, 1993.

Moore, Timothy J, *The Theatre of Plautus: Playing to the audience*. Austin: University of Texas Press, 1998.

Plautus, *Four Comedies*, translated by Erich Segal. Oxford: Oxford University Press, 1996.

Segal, Erich, *Roman Laughter: The Comedy of Plautus*. Oxford: Oxford University Press, 1987.

Terence

Harsh, Philip Whaley, *A Handbook of Classical Drama*. Stanford: Stanford University Press, 1944.

Terence, *Comedies*, translated by Betty Radice. Harmondsworth: Penguin Books, 1965.

Social background

Andrewes, Anthony, *Greek Society*. Harmondsworth: Penguin Books, 1971.

4.   DISCUSSION POINTS

- Discuss the connection the god Dionysus had with the Greek theatre and the plays staged in it.
- What changes were necessitated when the Greek theatre complex was adapted by the Romans?
- Do you think an 'archaeological' production of a Greek play would be acceptable to a modern British audience?
- What did *catharsis* mean to a Greek spectator? Does it have a meaning today?

- How did the intentions of Roman writers differ from those of Greek writers? Did these differences entail production modifications?
- Can we learn anything of religious, political and social life in fifth century Athens from the plays of this period?

5. NOTES AND REFERENCES

1 Sophocles, *Three Tragedies*, translated by H D F Kitto. London: Oxford University Press, 1962.

2 Howatson, M C and Ian Chilvers, eds, *The Oxford Concise Companion to Classical Literature*. Oxford: Oxford University Press, 1993.

3 The translation by Robert Fagles, published by Penguin Classics, has been used in this section.

4 Oliver Taplin, *Greek Tragedy in Action*. London: Routledge, 1978, p 39.

5 *Classical Literary Criticism*, ed Penelope Murray and T S Dorsche. Harmondsworth: Penguin Books, 1965, p 71.

6 The theatre at Sabratha is illustrated in Phyllis Hartnoll, *The Theatre: a Concise History*. London: Thames and Hudson, 1985, p 24.

ELIZABETHAN AND JACOBEAN ENGLAND

1.   SURVEY

The Mediaeval Stage

It is dawn on Easter morning in the great abbey church of Winchester which also served as the diocesan cathedral; as the third lesson is read, three monks detach themselves from the choir and make their way to an empty sepulchre in one of the transepts, wearing their long white albs and gold copes: they represent the three holy women looking for the body of the crucified Christ. When they arrive at the sepulchre they find two further monks standing there, personating the angels of the resurrection and a conversation ensues. 'Whom seek ye in the sepulchre, O Christian women?' the angels ask, getting the reply, 'Jesus of Nazareth, the crucified.' In turn the angels proclaim: 'He is not here. He is risen, as He foretold. Go and announce that he is risen from the dead.' Then the women turn to the monastic choir as the sun starts to filter through the window spaces, calling to the monks: 'Alleluia! The Lord is risen.'[1]

This is one of England's oldest plays, stemming from the tenth century; here is a mix of drama and liturgy with the choir, ostensibly the audience, joining in the dialogue. The material for the episode is taken from St Mark's gospel and indeed all the plays performed in the church building tended to be based on biblical records. Surrounding both monks and parishioners were the painted wall frescoes, the stained glass windows and the carvings on the west front of the abbey church which told the great and lengthy story of man's salvation beginning with the fall of the proud angel Lucifer, continuing through the creation of mankind, a narrative of the life of Christ and finishing with the account of the Last Judgement. Such cycles of plays were acted during the celebration of the Feast of Corpus Christi either within the church, outside at the west front or, as at York, in procession through the city at various 'stations' such as the gates cut within the walls. Only a few of the cycles are extant in whole or part: the *Ludus Coventriae* (the cycle for the city of Coventry), the York cycle, the Chester cycle and that of Wakefield. Plays were written for other festivals and were performed at salient points within the building, such as the story of the presentation of Mary in the Temple by Anne and Joachim her parents. Most suitably much of this was acted at the font, the place of the baptism and reception of Christians.

Gradually plays were removed from the church buildings – behaviour could be unseemly or the text inappropriate but often the sole reason was that the material was non-Biblical, although it had a moral purpose – to a variety of locations. Some of the strangest are the 'rounds' found in Cornwall, a raised circular bank within which a 'performance in the round' was given. *The Castel of Perseverance* that takes place around a tower, in which Mankind shelters, and on several scaffolds, a useful place for the Vices to stand and declaim, as well as employing a ditch, has been performed at Piran Round. Within the house, there were hall-plays, probably performed in front of the screens passage, using a platform between the two entrances and the gallery above the passage; *Everyman* is a morality ideally suited to such a location.

The Elizabethan Theatre

Inn yards

Arriving at the Elizabethan playhouses we see that there are many parallels with the mediaeval play locations, although in Elizabethan times churches were not generally used for productions. Inn yards were put to good use. From 1576 that of the Red Lion in Stepney was furnished with 'scaffolds', presumably for performing on. The ground of the yard was used by the plebs for watching the play – they stood – and the galleries served as a superior vantage point for people sitting on stools or chairs. The large, square yard of the Red Bull at Clerkenwell was converted from 1605 into a theatre and resembled the Red Lion by being open to the elements. Later users of this building were the Queen Anne's Men. It became a place renowned for its spectacular productions and owned a considerable amount of large scale ground rows of scenery. At a court proceedings after a disturbance we know from the report that oranges, apples and nuts were sold as refreshments.

The only galleried inn yard left in the City is that of the George Inn at Southwark which is still used for performances of Elizabethan plays.

Outdoor playhouses

Elizabethan theatres were to be found not within but outside the perimeter of the City, principally on Bankside, south of the river near London Bridge, where the Rose, the Hope, the Swan and the Globe were situated. This area was within the estate of the Bishop of Winchester, whose diocese then reached to the Thames and was famous for its brothels. To the north in Clerkenwell and Shoreditch, in addition to the Red Bull, were the Theatre and the Curtain. One had to travel to Whitechapel to attend the converted inns of the Boar's Head and the Red Lion. Let us look at a contrasting couple of these playhouses.

Little is known of the first Globe which burnt down in 1613 during a performance of *Henry VIII* when cannons set fire to the thatch of the tiring house roof. With the aid of public subscription and a royal grant the edifice was rebuilt and opened the following year. The second Globe is shown in Hollar's *Long View of London* (1647) but wrongly titled as the bear baiting pit. It is the usual 'wooden O' shape mentioned by the Chorus in *Henry V*. Very little is known of the tiring house façade, the building at the rear of the stage the audience would have gazed at during the course of the play. However, exterior stairways built against the walls led to the upper galleries.

Walter Hodges meticulously researched archive material and made a number of reconstructions of the second Globe. In these he proposed that there were three polygonal balconies, the first of which was situated at ground level and stepped upwards. He worked on the exact positioning of a thrust stage, backed by the tiring house. At stage level two entrances led onto the platform and an 'inner space' existed in front of which a curtain, the arras, hung. At the level of the second balcony a gallery ran across the back of the tiring house. It was possible to close in parts of this with curtains. Two massive columns rose from the stage and held aloft a canopy over the stage. This was surmounted in part by a thatched roof and also by the music room, home of the musicians, a small turret and the flag of the theatre. Already we gain an idea of the uses of some parts of the stage. The balcony could serve as that outside Juliet's bedroom in *Romeo and Juliet*. Because it was in shadow (one must remember that performances were given during the afternoons) it might also be the area of the battlements over which Hamlet's father's spectre walked. A flying apparatus was concealed out of sight in the canopy and this could be utilised for Puck (*A Midsummer Night's Dream*) and Ariel (*The Tempest*) as well as other non-mortal characters to wing into view. The inner room might well be the discovery area for the chess game in *The Tempest*, and also, used in conjunction with the main stage, the sanctum for Hermione's 'statue' (*The*

Winter's Tale). Whether it was used for complete scenes such as Gertrude's chamber (*Hamlet*) is a moot point. Later in the play the gravediggers prepare the ground for Ophelia's internment and the employment of one of a number of trap doors in the floor of the main stage was a likely device for this activity. There was no attempt at scenery: the stage was an unlocalised *platea* and any attempt at persuading the audience to picture the surrounding woods or buildings was by means of poetic descriptions.

The film version of *Henry V* in which Laurence Olivier played the title role gave impressions of the Globe Theatre and an accurate reconstruction close to the original site has been created by Sam Wanamaker.

A drawing is extant of the interior of another theatre, the Swan, made by a Dutch visitor, Johannes de Witt, some twenty years after his stay in London; a further remove is that the extant drawing has been copied by Arend van Buchell.[2] However, some purposes are served by it. Van Buchell refers to the building as the most magnificent and largest on the South Bank and claims that it holds three thousand people. There is a canopy over the rear part of the stage supported by wooden pillars painted to resemble marble. Unusually the drawing shows the stage raised up on legs. Van Buchell notes that the yard is unroofed. The tiring house is at the rear of the stage, a home for costumes and properties and also a changing place. The players entered through two large doors at the rear of the stage that might also have done service as a discovery space as references were made to an arras.[3] What we do miss in de Witts' drawing is an inner stage and also a trap letting down into the 'hell hole'. Six windows look out of the tiring house onto the stage and we are forced to ask, 'Is this a rehearsal going on with actors idly watching? Or is it a performance with the audience virtually surrounding the actors? Does one of the windows give onto the music room?' The suspension gear could have been installed beneath the flagpole in the loft.[4]

The Rose Theatre stood on Bankside in the Liberty of the Clink on the site of a former rose garden. Erected in 1587 it was the first purpose-built playhouse on Bankside, octagonal and made of wood and plaster on a brick foundation. Philip Henslowe, a local business man and dyer, built the theatre. His son-in-law and business partner was Edward Alleyn, one of the great actors of his day, establishing the principal roles in all of Marlowe's plays. Henslowe's diary gives an account of the plays staged. So successful an actor was Alleyn that when he retired he used part of his fortune to found The College of God's Gift, now popularly named Dulwich College, in south London. Archaeologists from the Museum of London discovered and excavated the site of the Rose in 1988–9 when the ground was being prepared for the construction of Rose Court, a new commercial building. A reconstruction of the Rose featured in the film *Shakespeare in Love.*

The principal companies

It is difficult to state with accuracy which companies acted regularly within which theatres. However, these are the principal companies paired with their known locations.

The Curtain, situated at Spitalfields, was probably used by the Lord Chamberlain's Company between 1597–9. James Burbage and William Shakespeare were members.

The company at the Rose from 1592 was Strange's Men and from 1594 the Lord Admiral's Men. From the first date the two companies intermittently joined forces but from 1594 Lord Strange's men went their own way, eventually returning to the provinces from whence they first appeared. The Admiral's Men seem to have been the first company to employ Shakespeare, either as actor or playwright, possibly both.

The Chamberlain's Men, headed by Richard Burbage, held sway at the Globe. Shakespeare was a 'Housekeeper' or holder of a share in the playhouse. As an open theatre it only presented plays in the summer; after 1613 accommodation during the winter was provided at the indoors Blackfriars Theatre.

Francis Langley, a London goldsmith, built the Swan and invited the Earl of Pembroke's company to perform regularly. A seditious play, *The Isle of Dogs*, was presented by the company in 1597, prompting the Privy Council to close public playhouses. Pembroke's men, together with those of the Earl of Sussex were mentioned on the title page of Shakespeare's *Titus Andronicus* (*c*.1590).

Indoor theatres: the second Blackfriars

The traditional octagonal playhouses had the disadvantage of being unsuitable, as they were open to the weather, for use during the winter. The solution would seem to be to build or adapt a rectangular roofed construction, a strategy in which Richard Burbage engaged when his Shoreditch playhouse, the Theatre, was twenty years old and in need of renewal. He selected part of the old Dominican conventual buildings at Blackfriars, the Parliament Chamber or Great Hall, one of the grandest buildings in the complex. A number of the features of the open-air buildings were adapted for use in the renovated premises. A tiring house, made possibly from the screen of the hall, offered a gallery approached by a ladder and in front of this was a thrust stage. Galleries at the sides and rear of the hall contained seating and benches stood facing the stage. Play texts of this period demand three doorways, each hung with curtains, and the facility for flying was a further requirement. Lighting would be artificial. The hall, 46 feet by 66 feet, made a noble playhouse, so that higher prices could be charged than in the open-air structures.

As soon as the building was prepared the residents of Blackfriars, fearful of noise and crowds, petitioned the Privy Council to ban the players partly because the Lord Chamberlain had apartments in the vicinity. However, acceptable tenants were found: the Children of the Chapel Royal and the choristers of St Paul's Cathedral would give performances in the Blackfriars' Hall. They performed there for eight years until 1608. Then it was acceptable for Burbage's company – known by that time as the King's Men – to take possession and there they remained until the closure of the theatres in 1642.

Elizabethan and Jacobean drama

The precursors

The Headmaster of Eton, and later of Westminster, Nicholas Udall, wrote and produced *Ralph Roister Doister* in 1553 for his boys to act. It was based on *Miles Gloriosus* by Plautus and in common with Roman plays used a five act structure. In it we meet some of the types of Roman and Tudor comedy: there is the braggart soldier, Ralph, and the journeying parasite, Merygreeke, the very English Widow Custance and her nurse Madge Mumblecrust. In the format of some of the mediaeval plays irregular rhyming couplets are the verse form. In addition to the dialogue there are songs, a mock-dirge and yokel farce, all of which seem to link the play with the Christmas Festival of Misrule.

Totally different is *The Tragedy of Mr Arden of Feversham*. This is as fresh as if the plot had just come off the front page of today's copy of *The Times* although it was published in 1592. The audience is presented with a documentary dramatisation of an actual murder which occurred in 1551 after a number of attempts, when Mistress Arden and her paramour Mosby killed Arden. The play is anonymous.

Christopher Marlowe

Marlowe was born in 1564, the same year as Shakespeare, but his career was cut short by his untimely death in 1593. After he left Cambridge, Marlowe wrote the two parts of *Tamburlaine the Great* (1587) followed by *The Jew of Malta* (1589) and *Dr Faustus* (1592). Tamburlaine is an ambitious tyrant with a great lust for power: this was brought home in the staging of Sir Donald Wolfitt's production at the Old Vic Theatre when the invader spread a map of the known world across the stage and proceeded to take enormous strides over the lands he planned to conquer. Faustus, a scholar and necromancer, tries to reach theological kingdoms by seeking after the unattainable in both personal lust and superhuman knowledge. Barabas, the Jew of Malta, is possessed by avarice, justifying from scripture his longing for gold and ultimately falling headlong into the fires of hell; he himself becomes part of the smelting process. Thus the principal character in each play is an overreacher, stretching beyond his abilities. In each there may well be something of Marlowe. The playwright was killed in a Deptford tavern by a dagger wound inflicted after a quarrel about the reckoning of a bill.

William Shakespeare: the plays

It must not be forgotten that Shakespeare was a working playwright, taking his turn on the stages of several Bankside theatres. There are three genres in which Shakespeare specialised; history plays, comedies and tragedies; although in his early work there is a clean-cut categorisation, the complexities of his later work often fog the boundaries. The most popular of the comedies are probably *A Midsummer Night's Dream* (1595), *Twelfth Night* (1601) and *The Merchant of Venice* (1596). A theme beyond the narrative line runs through each. *The Dream* is a study in romantic love, not only in typical lovers but in aristocratic courtiers, fairies (the Oberon, Titania and Bottom trio) and in the 'heroic' fictional characters the court is treated to in the interlude of 'Pyramus and Thisbe'. However, in *Twelfth Night* everyone is in love with himself or herself ('O, you are sick of self-love, Malvolio' says Olivia), a point made at Stratford one year when characters held personal hand-mirrors into which they adoringly looked.[5] Almost as if they are interludes, a number of external events embellish *The Merchant*: there is the business of the caskets, the antithetical symbolism of the rings, the love affair of Jessica and Lorenzo, a treatise on the morality of usury and a further one on the distinctiveness of the stranger – in this case the Jewish Shylock in a Christian city. Varied as these threads may be, they are woven with ease into the principal narrative.

Although several of the histories, such as the three parts of *Henry VI, King John* and *Henry V*, were written early in Shakespeare's career, we find a distinctive approach to the scale of history which will be explored later in this section.

About the year 1600 Shakespeare's work took on a darker hue. During the first decade of the seventeenth century he wrote his major tragedies, *Hamlet* (1602*)*, *Othello* (1604*)*, *Macbeth* (1606*)*, and *King Lear* (1605). Even the comedies, which some years earlier had been delightful, pastoral pieces set in enchanting woodlands and forests, became bitter: one has only to look at *Measure for Measure* (*c.*1602) and the 'comedy of disillusion', *Troilus and Cressida* (1602), to appreciate this. However, between 1608 and 1612 the tone of the comedies, although serious, changes. In *The Winter's Tale* (1611) there is the delightful world of shepherds and harvesting in the second half of the play to balance the jealousy of the first and the island world of magic in *The Tempest* (1611), often rumoured to be Shakespeare's farewell to the stage as Prospero speaks his valediction.

William Shakespeare: the themes

It may be helpful when you are reading a selection of Shakespeare's plays to consider the themes that he presents to his audiences. Several are selected at random here. First the theme of kingship appears, not solely in the history plays but also in others such as *King Lear*. Shakespeare, and he would not be alone here, views the king as the apex in a realm of the human species for he has been chosen by God and anointed with the holy oils. However great his failure in his duty as king – witness Richard II – any insurrection against him borders on regicide: it is no wonder that Bolingbroke, after usurping Richard's place and assuming the regalia as Henry IV, eventually becomes a broken man beneath the weight of the crown and, not restricted to one man, this malfeasance impinges on the subsequent dynasty. Here is one of the factors that fascinates Shakespeare, the variance between the exaltation of the royal office and the unworthiness of the man on whom the mantle is cast. In considering this in *Richard II* (1595) the playwright creates a scene in the Duke of York's garden in which the weeds and the parlous state of the kingdom are likened by the gardener's man to each other:

> ...our sea-walled garden, the whole land,
> Is full of weeds, her fairest flowers chok'd up,
> Her fruit-trees all unprun'd, her hedges ruin'd,
> Her knots disordered, and her wholesome herbs
> Swarming with caterpillars.   (Act 3, scene 4)

Metaphors used to describe the king normally employ a corresponding object in an appropriate set. Thus the sun, the light set at the apex of the stars and planets, is a just image for the king and ironically Richard uses this in relation to his usurper:

> God save King Henry, unking'd Richard says,
> And send him many years of sunshine days!
>   (Act 4, scene 1)

Even Richard the dreamer realises that political stability is an attribute of kingship in which every Elizabethan Englishman put his trust.

Blindness is a further theme employed to good effect by Shakespeare. It is most evident in the latter acts of *King Lear*. Often in the past Gloucester had been blind, not recognising in which of his two sons, the legitimate or the bastard, duty regulates action; in consequence of which, having mislaid discernment, he loses his sight, his eyes put out by Cornwall. What a macabre form of justice, for in his youth Gloucester sired an illegitimate child and the sign hanging outside the many brothels on Bankside was the Blind Cupid, the fat cherub with bandaged eyes.

The third theme I mention is that of the stranger, because there is a difference about any interloper, principally that he is 'not one of us', a political phrase used by Margaret Thatcher. A fascinating stranger in the canon is Shylock the Jew, alien not only by race but also by religion and by profession, although exactly what that constitutes is vague, a combination of law, usury and possibly butchery. Shakespeare is particularly skilful in suggesting that Shylock speaks differently from the Christians of Venice, a city that, perforce by trading, had opened its quays to all and sundry. Try reading aloud these few lines in which Shylock incorporates a number of voices:

> What should I say to you? Should I not say,
> 'Hath a dog money? Is it possible
> A cur can lend three thousand ducats?' Or
> Shall I bend low, and in a bondman's key,

> With bated breath and whisp'ring humbleness,
> Say this: 'Fair sir, you spat on me on Wednesday last…'
>
> (Act 1, scene 3)

Othello, the Moor of Venice, is a further citizen of that mysterious city who does not really fit, whereas Iago, scheming and complicitous, deftly moves amongst his neighbours. As with many Jacobean villains he is a character who hides amongst the shadows, silently surveying the world around him.

In *The Tempest* the strangers are travellers on three voyages, cast ashore on an imaginary island of geography and poetry during not one but three tempests: first there is Sycorax, the mother of Caliban, then Prospero, exiled from his native dukedom, Milan, and finally Alonso the usurper. We gain few glimpses of the true island inhabitants. Ariel is one who belongs although he has obviously been colonised by Prospero, there are the goddesses such as Ceres and Juno, and the sprites who appear with the cornucopia which is such a disappointment to those who snatch at the feast.

Short as these notes are, perhaps these three examples of Shakespeare's choice of themes is helpful in keeping a watch for others.

William Shakespeare: the life

William Shakespeare's father John came from Snitterfield, a town situated between Stratford and Warwick and a more prestigious place than the present village suggests even though its position in the Forest of Arden made it somewhat remote. John moved to Henley Street in Stratford sometime before 1552, buying two adjoining houses there, one for living in and the other where he pursued his line of business which seems to have consisted of selling meat and making and selling gloves and additionally leather and wool. Shakespeare's mother, Mary Arden, lived in a spacious farmhouse in Wilmcote, a small churchless village four miles from Stratford. She, of course, joined John in Stratford at their marriage. At the Henley Street house in 1564 William Shakespeare was born, he was baptised at the magnificent Church of the Holy Trinity, attended the Grammar School in Chapel Street and seems to have helped his father in the business. Possibly he occasionally made the journey over the fields to Shottery where a woman eight years his senior lived; she was Anne Hathaway and when the couple discovered that she was pregnant, in 1582, they married; William was eighteen years old.

At this point in his life Shakespeare journeyed to London. By 1594 he was a leading member of the Lord Chamberlain's Men. Although London was his professional base, the family continued to live at Stratford. Possibly the writer often returned for in 1597 he bought a large house, New Place with its attractive gardens, opposite the Falcon tavern in Chapel Street. When James VI of Scotland became James I of England in 1603, the Chamberlain's Men became the King's Men. They were a company of some stature for they not only held the Globe Theatre but the king provided nine named King's Men with a length of red material from which the royal livery could be made.

By 1608 Shakespeare may have made a partial retirement from London theatre life; he nevertheless bought a gatehouse close to the Blackfriars theatre. The inscription on his monument in Holy Trinity Church tells us that he died in April 1616 and was interred in the church, the first of the Shakespeare family to lie there.

From the middle of the nineteenth century some literary critics developed the Baconian Theory in which it was postulated that Shakespeare's plays were in fact written by Sir Francis Bacon, first Baron Verulam. The reasoning behind the speculation is that:

- Only a person of superior education and knowledge would be capable of creating such complex works.
- The obscurity of Shakespeare's life mitigates against the plays having been written by him.
- External circumstances (a father who was a tradesman and a family in which some members were unable to write) also points to a writer with a more advanced education, such as a graduate or a member of the Inns of Court.

It has to be admitted that most of the proponents of the theory were not scholars with a lasting reputation although amongst them were Lord Penzance, Sir Theodore Martin and Sir G Greenwood.

Ben Jonson

Ben Jonson was both an admirer and a stern critic of Shakespeare whose work he regarded as undisciplined. Jonson is annoyed that a writer should attempt

> To make a child, now swaddled to proceed
> Man, and then shoot up, in one beard, and weed,
> Past three score years...[6]

Here is a contemptuous allusion to the writing of Shakespeare's histories; Shakespeare's work lacks classical form. He is looking for a recognisable truth in the world around the playhouse, those sordid London streets in the Liberty of the Clink, and wants to hear

> Deeds and language such as men do use,
> And persons such as comedy would choose
> When she would show an image of the times.

In Jonson's day 'humour' was a medical word denoting a propensity or affection. The character of a person was thought to be determined by a ruling humour, one of four physiological elements, blood, choler, phlegm or melancholy. A perfect disposition could only be achieved if there were a balanced mix of these.

Volpone (1605) opens with a statement from the bearer of the title role: a greed for gold is the great allure within his life. As Volpone arises from his bed, he directs Mosca, his parasite, to open the 'shrine' that he may worship his wealth stored therein. The setting of the play – the bedroom on a larger scale – is Venice, one of the most magnificent treasures of the Adriatic and yet Jonson's characters are each named after a creature of prey: Voltore (a vulture), Corbaccio (a raven), Corvino (a crow) and Volpone the fox.

Most of Jonson's other plays are set on home ground and here one may meet the world of scavengers found on the doorstep of the playhouse. In and around Lovewit's house at Blackfriars is the setting for *The Alchemist* (1610), where, in the absence of Lovewit the servants attempt to fleece a variety of outlandish callers such as Sir Epicure Mammon and the fanatical puritan Tribulation Wholesome, a fine use of 'humours' names. They offer visitors the chance to possess the famous Philosopher's Stone ('This is the famous stone /That turneth all to gold,' wrote George Herbert); these visitors arrive one by one in the early morning as they do in *Volpone* and it is obvious that Jonson is influenced by the Roman habit of making one's courtesy calls as early as possible in the day.

Bartholomew Fair (1614) is a prose comedy rather than one in verse; even so, whilst watching a London revival Kenneth Tynan opined that to stand up the play needed crutches.[7] It seems to have little shape and yet it is one of the great London documentaries and as such its gallery of rogues has to be seen, appreciated and allowed to pass by without a hint of a moral message. For some this is an omission. For example L C Knights complains:

> *Epicoene*… (1609) and, I think, *Bartholomew Fair* (1614) belong to the category of stage entertainments: in them the fun is divorced from any rich significance – though many would disagree with this verdict on *Bartholomew Fair.* [8]

Three Jacobean plays

With a slow progress James VI of Scotland travelled to London to become James I of England after the death of Queen Elizabeth I in 1603. Much was to change. James, with his speech impediment, found communication difficult. His interest in the occult and witchcraft and his demonstrative homosexuality together with his catholic tendencies were an offence to many. Furthermore he was a spendthrift: an expensive foreign policy and an extravagant court at home bit into the exchequer. Confrontation with Parliament was inevitable.

Three Jacobean dramas give a flavour of the change in playwriting that coincided with the reigns of James and Charles I: *The Duchess of Malfi* (1612–4) by John Webster; *The Changeling* (1622) by Thomas Middleton and William Rowley; and *'Tis Pity She's a Whore* (1627) by John Ford. The first of these is a she-tragedy in which the title role and central character is no longer a male person (such as Hamlet, Othello or Macbeth) but a woman, furthermore one played by an actress rather than a boy. The plot is based on actuality: the characters lived a century before Webster's day and the duchess was Giovanna d'Aragona, married at the age of twelve to the heir to the dukedom of Amalfi who died young, from gout. Loneliness drove her to a secret marriage with the *major-domo* of the king of Naples, Antonio Bologna. As in

Webster's play the Cardinal of Aragon was Giovanna's brother. Several versions of the history of the Duchess were extant at the time Webster composed his tragedy.

A number of themes run through the play which may be found in other tragedies too. There is the corruption of princely courts; the different ways in which nobility faces death; and the question, 'Why was the Duchess killed?' The effect of her death is to spotlight her virtue: 'I am Duchess of Malfi still.' (Act IV, scene 2), she says, emphasising her dignity in the face of adversity. Thereby the murderous intentions of the Cardinal, Ferdinand and Bosola are pushed back into the shadows where much of the action takes place, especially in the fourth act, a great chamber of horrors.

The audience gradually becomes fascinated by the single-mindedness of Bosola in *The Duchess* and there is a similar effect in *The Changeling*. Here the servant De Flores is the counterpart of Bosola; he is hired by Beatrice to eliminate her fiancé, Alonso de Piraquo, of an arranged marriage, so that she may marry Alsemero whom she lusts after. The guilty in the subsequent murder are discovered and poison themselves. The sub-plot (a study in madness) has little connection with the main one – and, in fact, the two plots only converge at a couple of points – although the play's title is taken from the sub-plot, Antonio the changeling. This is a term simply referring to the substitution of one infant for another by the fairies but in the harsh world of Jacobean tragedy it is applied to a fickle person who is exchanged for another; substitution is one of the themes running through *The Changeling*. As in Shakespeare's late tragedies, the ghosts of murdered men appear at inconvenient junctures in the narration.

'Tis Pity She's a Whore is a Caroline drama, yet the tenor of the writing belongs to the early Jacobean

tragedies. John Ford was educated at the Middle Temple in London and afterwards probably practised law in some form; his literary output seems to begin in 1606 with the publication of some minor prose and verse works. In *'Tis Pity* Ford takes the audience to Parma, governed by a scion of the Habsburg family who preserved its wealth by inbreeding. Giovanni has an unnatural, sexual love for his sister Annabella whom he makes pregnant but the play is not a pleading for wider acceptances; instead it is the presentation of star-crossed lovers, similar to Romeo and Juliet, in which the suffering of a noble family is presented for consideration. Time and again Ford places before us a subject that is unpalatable and yet uses a sensitive dialogue in relation to it:

> Brother, dear brother, know that I have been,
> And know that now there's but a dining-time
> 'Twixt us and our confusion.

L G Salingar notes that Ford maintains the plot mechanisms of Shakespeare's day: in *'Tis Pity* after Giovanni has murdered his sister he appears to the diners at Soranzo's banquet with her heart 'upon his dagger' before killing the man to whom she has been betrothed.[9]

Elizabethan, Jacobean and Caroline Poetry

During the Elizabethan and Jacobean periods one of the most popular poetic forms was the sonnet and one of the greatest sequences of these was written by William Shakespeare. Two hundred years earlier an Italian priest, Francesco Petrarch, had established a pattern for the sonnet; Shakespeare altered this. He maintained the fourteen lines but, because of the paucity of English rhyming words, he adopted a different placement for these. As an example, let us look at Shakespeare's Sonnet 18:

Shall I compare thee to a summer's day?
Thou art more lovely and more temperate;
Rough winds do shake the darling buds of May,
And summer's lease hath all too short a date;
Sometimes the eye of heaven shines,
And often is his gold complexion dimm'd:
And every air from fair sometimes declines,
By chance, or nature's changing course untrimm'd;
But thy eternal summer shall not fade,
Nor lose possession of that fair thou ow'st,
Nor shall death brag thou wander'st in his shade,
When in eternal lines to time thou grow'st;
    So long as men can breathe, or eyes can see,
    So long lives this, and this gives life to thee.

What comment would you make on the shape of the poem established by the rhyming words? If we use a series of letters for like-rhyming words at the end of lines we discover the following pattern:

A B A B C D C D E F E F G G

The sonnet is made up of three stanzas, each of four lines (a quatrain). Within each stanza, line 1 rhymes with line 3 and line 2 with line 4. The last stanza consists of only two lines – a rhyming couplet – rounding off the piece.

Shakespeare is eager that the pattern of the sonnet (sometimes referred to as 'the form') should support the meaning of what he is saying. Generally the meaning fits easily into the form.

- Often in the first quatrain there is an opening proposition. Sonnet 18 opens with a question: 'Shall I compare thee to a summer's day?' Then follows a list of difficulties related to the proposition: the person addressed is 'more lovely' than a day in summer, rough winds

> spoil the May buds and summer lasts a very
> short time with the effect that the beauty of
> the flowers are soon spent.

- The next four lines (5–8) continue the
  objections to the simile.
- On arriving at line 9 a change comes over the
  sonnet. The first word of this line is 'But'. A
  contradiction ensues and the sonnet becomes
  more positive about the many qualities of the
  Earl of Southampton, for it is he who is said to
  be the subject of the sonnet.

This brief word 'But' helps us to realize that we can
recognize another pattern in the form.

- The first eight lines may be taken as a whole,
  all depending on the opening simile: we refer
  to this block of the poem as the 'octet'.
- The remaining six lines form the sestet,
  complete with the contradiction of ideas and
  the two line summary at the end.

In dealing with the technicalities of the sonnet the metre and
the rhythm must be kept in mind as well as the above
rhyming scheme. Shakespeare writes his sonnets in iambic
pentameters. An iambic foot is one which has a |weak,
strong| rhythm. The word 'pentameter' suggests that there
are five such feet in a line and thereby five strong beats also
run through each line:

> |weak, strong| weak, strong| weak, strong| weak,
> strong| weak, strong|

Shakespeare, however, does not use the metre in a
mechanical way and often one finds at the beginning of a line
that he has inverted the first foot, giving us a different pattern
which changes our appreciation of what is said. An instance

occurs in Sonnet 29 in which, for good measure, inversions occur in the line before the one that is given the initial thrust:

> Yet in these thoughts myself almost despising,
> Haply I think on thee...

Hopefully it is clear that the Shakespearean sonnet is a sophisticated way of thinking about a subject encased in a fairly rigid structure.

There is room only to mention three other writers of this period: Edmund Spenser, John Donne and John Milton. Edmund Spenser was born about 1552; after a Cambridge education he was appointed secretary to the governor of Ireland where he remained for the rest of his life. His major work is *The Faerie Queen* (1589 and 1596), a complex epic celebrating the glory of England and her ruler. He has been accused in the past of over-complicating the allegory, packing too much on to the back of each character: King Arthur, for example, represents Magnificence, he is also the symbol for divine grace, there is in him a suggestion of Lord Leicester, Elizabeth's favourite, and finally he is in love with the Faerie Queen. This complexity also muddies the narrative line. In Book One the adventures of the Red Cross Knight represent, sometimes in turn and at others simultaneously, the Christian in search of truth, the alternatives offered by Protestantism and Roman Catholicism, and the ebb and flow of faith in the sixteenth century. Spenser's strength is in word-painting: in the allegory there are elaborate descriptions of tapestries and paintings, some of which, such as 'The Wedding of the Thames and the Medway', are on a gigantic scale, and it can be maintained that at times Spenser forgets the symbolical and moral meaning of these word master-pieces. The *masque* at this time was enjoying a period of popularity and Spenser was obviously captivated by this. We get an idea of what these were like in Inigo Jones's designs in the collection at Chatsworth House in Derbyshire and we can see the masque in operation in the sub-plot of *The Changeling*. Much of *The Faerie Queen* is in the nature of a masque with its changing scenery, groupings of actors and dancers and their pantomimic performance. For example, Spenser gets totally caught up in his descriptions of each character of the months of the year:

> Then came faire May, the fayrest mayd on ground,
> Deckt all with dainties of her seasons pryde,
> And throwing flowers out of her lap around
> (Book VII, Canto VII, xxxiv)

The illusion that the poem is accompanied by music is achieved by Spenser's use of the nine-line stanza held together by the elaborate and limited rhyming scheme:

A B A B B C B C C

The five stresses of each line mount to a six-stress line (the Alexandrine) every time the final line of the stanza returns, giving a heavy sonority to the overall sound.

Coming to the end of reading this enormous work, C S Lewis, then a teenager, wept as he realised that there was no more to follow: in adult life Lewis wrote one of the most popular and enthusiastic commentaries on the poem in *The Allegory of Love* (1936). In Spenser Lewis had found a kindred spirit, for both were bookish. Simply to read a few stanzas of this monumental work gives one an impression of the genius of the poet. Two other works, both marriage songs, ought to be mentioned: these are *Epithalamion* (1594) and *Prothalamion* (1596).

There are two John Donnes, although his conversion was a gradual process rather than a Damascus road experience: the first is the man who wrote such poems as 'The Sunne Rising' with its references to his mistress with whom he is lying in bed, as the sum total of all things; and the second, the cleric who became Dean of St Paul's Cathedral in London and, again in bed, wrote of his physicians as 'Cosmographers' – natural scientists or geographers – pouring over the map of his dying body. The language of Donne's poetry is harsh, everyday and without poetic pretension. In 'The Good Morrow' he speaks to his mistress about where the pair bedded down before they met: '...snorted we in the seven sleepers den?', an intellectual note on the Christians of Ephesus who fled from the persecution of Decius and slept in a cavern for 187 years. His versification tends to be harsh and the images he uses are not poetic. One of his songs begins with a series of imperatives:

> Goe, and catch a falling starre,
> Get with child a mandrake roote...

The second injunction is weird: the mandrake root, because of its long tubular shape was seen as a male organ, that which would do the getting of the child rather than a passive recipient. Such instances could be repeated many times over. 'The most heterogeneous ideas,' wrote Samuel Johnson, are used so often and to such effect that they 'are yoked by violence together', ready for the term 'conceit' to be applied to them.[10] A group of poets grew up around Donne amongst whom may be counted George Herbert, Richard Crashaw, Andrew Marvell and Henry Vaughan. All are fascinating for verse speakers to wrestle with.

At Cambridge John Milton's poetic life was formed, at first with the intention of his becoming a clergyman but by the time he had gained his master's degree the lure of Anglicanism had weakened. Three phases in the development of commonwealth and post-commonwealth England co-incided with Milton's literary life. The first was the period prior to the protectorate when Charles I ruled.

At this time Milton was writing his lyric and elegiac poems and three fairly short poems are worthy of note: 'The Ode on the Morning of Christ's Nativity' (1629), 'Il Penseroso' (1632) and 'L'Allegro' (1632). The landscape of the two latter poems is a reflection of Milton's mind: pleasure for him is the balance of mirth and gravity. The Penseroso is a thinker in his high and lonely tower, a man who has rejected the playhouse for the Gothic cathedral. After being forsaken by his first wife Milton, the figure of the title, falls in love with Melancholy.

During the Commonwealth period (1642–60) Milton turned from poetry to polemical prose. By the Restoration Milton had become blind but, in spite of the difficulties of transcribing, this was the period of his greatest works, *Paradise Lost* (1667), *Paradise Regained* (1671) and *Samson Agonistes* (1671). The choice of theme for *Paradise Lost* did not come easily to Milton for at first he toyed with the idea of writing an Arthurian epic but the Hebrew scriptures dictated that the central figure in his chosen Genesis story was Man. An amount of rearrangement of the narrative was necessary and one sees a reworking of parts of the mediaeval mystery cycles. The casting out from Heaven of the rebel angels begins the epic, they plan a revenge in Hell, there is Satan's flight, man's temptation and fall from grace and finally the promise of redemption. Milton projects onto this scheme his own philosophy about the purpose of human existence; he attempts 'to justify the ways of God to men'. Whilst Man is the hero, the villain is Satan, a fascinating character who influenced drawings by the artists and writers of the Romantic movement.

Neither events nor the lives of writers fit happily into boxes and the latter part of this survey falls into the period covered by the next chapter. It would therefore be wise to look at the relevant sections of that survey, in order to obtain as complete an understanding as possible.

2.   SELECTED AUTHORS, PLAYWRIGHTS AND WORKS OF THE ELIZABETHAN AND JACOBEAN PERIOD

Note: Play titles are prefixed by an asterisk

1553:   *Ralph Roister Doister by Nicholas Udall

    1558:   Accession of Queen Elizabeth I

    1587:   Mary, Queen of Scots beheaded

1587:   *Tamburlaine the Great by Christopher Marlowe

1589:   The Faerie Queen, part 1 by Edmund Spenser

1589:   *The Jew of Malta by Christopher Marlowe

1591:   *Richard III by William Shakespeare

1592:   *Arden of Faversham, author unknown

1592:   *Dr Faustus by Christopher Marlowe

    1593:   The murder of Christopher Marlowe in Deptford

1594:   *Love's Labours Lost by William Shakespeare

1594:   Epithalamion by Edmund Spenser

1595:   *Richard II by William Shakespeare

1595:   *A Midsummer Night's Dream by William Shakespeare

1596:   *The Merchant of Venice by William Shakespeare

1596:   Prothalamion by Edmund Spenser

1596:   The Faerie Queen, part 2 by Edmund Spenser

1599:   *Henry V by William Shakespeare

    1599:   The first Globe Theatre opened on Bankside

1601:   *Twelfth Night by William Shakespeare

    1603:   Death of Elizabeth I; the union of England and Scotland; James VI of Scotland crowned James I of England

    1605:   The Gunpowder Plot

1605:   The Red Bull Tavern, Clerkenwell, revamped as a theatre

1605:   *King Lear by William Shakespeare

1606:   *Volpone by Ben Jonson

1606:   *Macbeth by William Shakespeare

1607:   *The Knight of the Burning Pestle by Francis Beaumont

1612–4: *The Duchess of Malfi by John Webster

1613:   The first Globe Theatre destroyed by fire

1614:   *Bartholomew Fair by Ben Jonson

1614:   *The Duchess of Malfi by John Webster

1614:   The second Globe Theatre opened on Bankside

1614:   John Donne ordained priest

1621:   John Donne appointed Dean of St Paul's Cathedral, London

1622:   *The Changeling by Thomas Middleton and William Rowley

1625:   Death of James I and accession of Charles I

1631:   Death of John Donne

c. 1632: Il Penseroso and L'Allegro by John Milton

1633:   *'Tis Pity She's a Whore by John Ford

1642:   The English Civil War begins, 1642–60, and the closure of the theatres

1644:   The second Globe Theatre demolished

1660:   The Restoration of Charles II to the throne of England

1667:   Paradise Lost by John Milton

1671:   *Samson Agonistes by John Milton

3.   BIBLIOGRAPHY

Mediaeval drama

Beadle, Richard and King, Pamela M, eds., *York Mystery Plays: A Selection in Modern Spelling*. Oxford: Oxford University Press, 1984.

Denny, Neville, ed., *Mediaeval Drama: Stratford upon Avon Studies, 16*. London: Edward Arnold, 1973.

Happé, Peter, *Medieval English Drama*. Harmondsworth: Penguin Books, 1984.

Richardson, Christine and Johnston, Jackie, *Medieval Drama*. Basingstoke: Macmillan, 1991.

Southern, Richard, *Mediaeval Theatre in the Round*. London: Faber and Faber, 1957.

The Elizabethan playhouse

Edwards, Christopher, ed., *The London Theatre Guide: 1576–1642*. London: The Bear Gardens Museum and Arts Centre, 1979.

Graham, Clare, 'Phoenix at the Rose' in *Speech & Drama*, 50 (Spring, 2001), 41–8.

Gurr, Andrew, *The Shakespeare Stage, 1574–1642*. Cambridge: Cambridge University Press, third edn. 1992.

Hodges, C Walter, *The Globe Restored*. London: Oxford University Press, 1968.

Hotson, Leslie, *Shakespeare's Wooden O*. London: Hart-Davis, 1959.

Linnell, Rosemary, *The Curtain Playhouse*. London: Curtain Theatre Publications, 1977.

Sisson, Charles J, 'Shakespeare's London' in *Shakespeare: A Celebration*, ed, T J B Spencer, Harmondsworth: Penguin Books, 1984.

Critical works: William Shakespeare

Clemen, W H, *The Development of Shakespeare's Imagery*. London: Methuen [1951].

Coghill, Nevill, *Shakespeare's Professional Skills*. Cambridge: Cambridge University Press, 1964.

Ford, Boris, ed., *The Pelican Guide to English Literature: The Age of Shakespeare*. Harmondsworth: Penguin Books, 1955.

Knight, G Wilson, *The Wheel of Fire: Interpretations of Shakespearean Tragedy*. London: Methuen, 1972.

Knights, L C, *Some Shakespeare Themes*. London: Chatto and Windus, 1959.

Righter, Anne, *Shakespeare and the Idea of the Play*. Harmondsworth: Penguin Books, 1967.

Thomson, Peter, *Shakespeare's Professional Career*. Cambridge: Cambridge University Press, 1992.

Tillyard, E M W, *The Elizabethan World Picture*. Harmondsworth: Penguin Books, 1963.

Wain, John, *The Living World of Shakespeare*. Harmondsworth: Penguin Books, 1964.

The Baconian Theory

Michel, J, *Who Wrote Shakespeare?* London: Thames and Hudson.

Schoenbaum, S, *Shakespeare's Lives*. 1970.

Critical works: other playwrights

Barish, Jonas, *Ben Jonson and the Language of Prose Comedy*. Cambridge, Mass: Harvard University Press, 1960.

Boas, F S, *Christopher Marlowe: A Biography and Critical Study*. Oxford: Clarendon Press, 1953.

Bogard, Travis, *The Tragic Satire of John Webster*. Berkeley and Los Angeles: University of California Press, 1955.

Bradbrook, M C, *Themes and Conventions of Elizabethan Tragedy*. Cambridge: Cambridge University Press, 2nd edition, 1980.

Ellis-Fermor, Una, *The Jacobean Drama*. London: Methuen, 1965.

Knights, L C, *Drama and Society in the Age of Jonson*. London: Methuen, 1977.

Lomax, Marion, *Stage Images and Traditions: Shakespeare to Ford*. Cambridge: Cambridge University Press, 1987.

Mulryne, J R, '*The White Devil* and *The Duchess of Malfi*' in John Russell Brown and Bernard Harris, *Stratford upon Avon Studies 1: Jacobean Theatre*. London: Arnold, 1965.

Partridge, E B, *The Broken Compass: A Study of the Major Comedies of Ben Jonson*. Westport, Conn: Greenwood, 1976.

Schoenbaum, S, *Middleton's Tragedies*. New York: Columbia University Press, 1955.

Wilson, Edmund, 'Morose Ben Jonson' in *Ben Jonson; A Collection of Critical Essays*, ed. J A Barish. Eaglewood Cliffs, Prentice Hall, 1963.

Woolf, V S, *Collected Essays*. London: Chatto and Windus, 1967 (contains an essay on John Ford).

Wymer, R, *Webster and Ford*. Basingstoke: Macmillan, 1995.

Biography

Donne, John

Gosse, Edmund, *The Life and Letters of John Donne*. London: W Heinemann, 1899.

Jonson, Ben

Bryant, J A, Jr, *The Compassionate Satirist: Ben Jonson and His Imperfect World*. Athens: University of Georgia Press, 1972.

Partridge, E B, *The Broken Compass*. Westport, Conn: Greenwood, 1976.

Shakespeare, William

Gurr, Andrew, *William Shakespeare*. London: HarperCollins Publishers, 1995.

Parker, Michael St John, *William Shakespeare*. London: Pitkin Pictorials, 1990, rep. 1994.

Schoenbaum, S, *William Shakespeare: A Compact Documentary Life*. New York and Oxford: Oxford University Press, 1987.

Webster, John

Bradbrook, M C, *John Webster: Citizen and Dramatist*. London: Weidenfeld and Nicolson, 1980.

Jacobean and Caroline Theatre

Bentley, G E, *The Jacobean and Caroline Stage*. Oxford: 1956.

Elizabeth, Jacobean and Caroline Poetry

Evans, J M, *Paradise Lost and the Genesis Tradition*. Oxford: Clarendon Press, 1968.

Gardner, Helen, ed, *The Metaphysical Poets*. Harmondsworth: Penguin Books, 1957.

Leishman, J B, *The Monarch of Wit*. London: Hutchinson, 1962.

Lewis, C S, *The Allegory of Love*. Oxford: Oxford University Press [1995].

Potter, L, *A Preface to Milton*. Harlow: Longman, 2000.

Renwick, W L, *Edmund Spenser: An Essay on Renaissance Poetry*. London: Methuen, 1964.

Sherwood, T G, *Fulfilling the Circle: A Study of John Donne's Thought*. Toronto and London: University of Toronto Press, 1984.

4.   DISCUSSION POINTS

- To what extent are the writings of William Shakespeare a mirror of his times?

- What changes do you perceive as Elizabethan drama moves to Jacobean drama? Try to account for them.

- How does Shakespeare use the Elizabethan theory of kingship in some of his plays?

- Take one of the plays you have studied and outline your ideas for a stage production.

- What are the distinctive elements an Elizabethan, a post-Restoration and a modern actor would confront in the theatre of these periods?

- Take a poet of this period and introduce him in context to a study group.

5. NOTES AND REFERENCES

1 From *The Concordia Regularis of Saint Ethelwold* and reproduced in A M Nagler, ed., *A Source Book in Theatrical History*. New York: Dover Publications, Inc., 1952.

2 The original drawing is in Arend van Buchell's commonplace book in the University Library, Utrecht.

3 Christopher Edwards, ed., *The London Theatre Guide, 1576–1642*. London: The Bear Gardens Museum, 1979, p. 23.

4 S Schoenbaum, *William Shakespeare. A Compact Documentary Life*. New York and Oxford: Oxford University Press, 1987. Bridges Adams, *Shakespearean Playhouses*, pp. 167–8.

5 *Twelfth Night*, Act 1, scene 5.

6 Jonson, prologue to *Every Man in His Humour*.

7 Tynan, *Curtains*, 1961, p. 3.

8 L C Knights, 'Ben Jonson, Dramatist' in Boris Ford, ed., *The Penguin Guide to English Literature: The Age of Shakespeare*. Harmondsworth: Penguin Books, 1955, p. 314.

9 L G Salingar, 'The Decline of Tragedy' in Ford, ed., *The Age of Shakespeare*, p. 439.

10 Johnson, Samuel, *The Life of Cowley*, 1779.

THE COMMONWEALTH AND RESTORATION STAGE

1. SURVEY

The Commonwealth Period

Charles I, a firm believer in the divine right of kings, battled with Parliament on constitutional and religious issues and the spending of state funds: this tug of war was the confrontation of a catholic outlook with puritan thought and economy. In 1642 there was an eruption and the Civil War followed. Charles was beheaded outside the Banqueting Hall of the partially built Palace of Whitehall, a magnificent room used later for the presentation of pageants. Oliver Cromwell – leader of the anti-Royalists – held parliament and the government of the realm together by force of a commanding personality until his death in 1658.

A new seriousness pervaded the atmosphere that Britain breathed and yet, in spite of attempts to eradicate the frivolity of entertainment, actors treated audiences to shows. The ten or so London theatres of Caroline days still stood, some in partial disrepair but good enough to house spectators as they watched revivals of formerly popular plays such as the works of Shakespeare or Beaumont and Fletcher. There were also cut-downs of plays, known as drolls, providing new amusements: an example is *Bottom the Weaver*, a bag of scraps taken from the subplot of *A Midsummer Night's Dream*. Two collections of drolls are extant: *The Wits* (published in 1662, incidentally the year of the publication of *The Book of Common Prayer*) and *The Stroler's Pacquet Open'd* (1742). Actors, as much as texts, also formed links with past days. George Jolly formed a company of players and took them to perform regularly in Germany. Another company was formed by

William Beeston whose father had known Shakespeare in the latter part of the Stratfordian's life. A further acting link was Sir William Davenant, the godson – some claimed natural son – of William Shakespeare. Towards the end of the Commonwealth period Davenant's opera *The Siege of Rhodes* (1656) and several other pieces were performed. In these music rather than theatre helped to make the entertainments acceptable.

The Restoration theatre building

Charles II, living in continental exile, was well accustomed to theatre buildings with a proscenium arch and a heavy green curtain hiding the scenic area of the stage. Long vistas and elaborate machinery gave the drama visual splendour and the presence of actresses provided a pleasure rarely experienced in earlier days in England. Practical scholarship was the king's forte; he spoke French fluently and understood Spanish and Italian. Above all, he was youthful and, if asked, agreed he would arrive in England with a court retinue. Two years after the death of Cromwell in 1660 the army invited Charles to return to his true home and rule from the English throne.

Disappointment must have been evident in theatrical circles when it was learnt that the king would grant patents to only two managers, Thomas Killigrew and Sir William Davenant. Davenant was the son of an Oxford tavern keeper and later leader of a company of players, the Duke's Men (that is, the acting company of the Duke of York). Killigrew, whose company was titled the King's Men, used the shell of a racquets court in Vere Street to set up his playhouse but of his alterations next to nothing is known. For his part Davenant adapted Lisle's Tennis Court in Portugal Street, Lincoln's Inn Fields, and for the opening production he selected an expanded version of *The Siege of Rhodes*. Before long Davenant commissioned Sir Christopher Wren to design the Duke's Theatre, Dorset Garden (south of Fleet Street) but in 1668 during the constructing of it Davenant died.[1]

Killigrew in the meantime had transferred his players to Bridges Street off Drury Lane and when his base burnt down in 1672 he also selected Wren to design him a theatre in Drury Lane on a site 112 feet long by 59 feet wide. The present Theatre Royal, Drury Lane is on the same site. The Duke's Theatre eventually changed location also. Davenant's patent, passing through family hands, came into the possession of John Rich who built the Theatre Royal, Covent Garden on land owned by the Duke of Bedford; this theatre opened in 1732. Before we consider the audiences who filled these two theatres, the building put up during the Restoration period deserves a brief description.

Wren's Drury Lane opened in 1674. At the ground level of the auditorium was a sloping pit containing ten rows of benches, curved so that they matched the curve of the theatre's forestage. A corridor ran from the entrance front of the house to the front of the pit and from here one selected a seat. Obviously, this pit passage was a fire hazard, quickly in an emergency becoming jammed with people. On either side of the auditorium and front-stage six great pilasters were set up between the two lines of boxes; instead of the final two first level boxes, proscenium doors led on to the stage. Through these the majority of entrances and exits were made. At the back of the theatre, facing the stage, were three balconies of seats – the inevitable and uncomfortable benches – and each balcony contained four rows of them. Patrons reached the balconies from a series of staircases stemming from the front entrance. There was a continuous sloping ceiling running from above the front of the balcony line to the rear of the forestage. Professor Richard Southern calculated that the building would hold in the region of eight hundred people.[2] Several times the forestage has been mentioned: what was its function? This was the area on which the play was performed by the cast. There was a further stage behind a proscenium arch on which an indication of the setting was given, usually painted on a couple of back shutters which could be slid apart by 'carpenters' wearing gloves as a protection against finger marks. At the sides would be up to seven wing pieces on which was painted a neutral subject such as columns, pilasters or swagged curtains and, of course, these would not need changing, they merely served to hide the wing-space. The orchestra was situated, often at floor level, in a roped-off area at the front of the pit. An earlier variant of this practice existed in the Duke's Theatre, Dorset Gardens, where the orchestra was in a small room above the proscenium arch; shutters and curtains divided it from the main part of the house. A more detailed description with suggested examples of the use of scenery is given in the following chapter; Rich's Covent Garden of 1732 also properly belongs here.

The courtly and the plebian audience

As the Restoration actor stood on the forestage and looked out front at his audience he recognised its major components: the town, the City and the Court.[3] Of these three, for a decade after Charles II's coronation, the court was the most important. Not only Davenant and Killigrew but also many dramatists were known personally to the king, writers such as John Dryden, the Duke of Buckingham, George Etherege, William Wycherley and John Crowne. Naturally the king was the arbiter of taste and soon influenced his surrounding courtiers. Killigrew observed to Pepys that, with the 'city audience' of the earlier Elizabethan playhouse well nigh gone, the tone of the theatre was much improved. However, contemporary reports suggest that the playhouse audience was not solely educated and literate. But had Killigrew summed up the social change accurately? In *The Young Gallant's Academy* by Samuel Vincent it is asserted that 'the Playhouse is free for entertainment, allowing Room as well to the Farmer's Son as to a Templer' or member of the Inns of Court. Pepys himself complains at times that the house is 'full of citizens'. To what extent is the audience attentive to the dramatist's work? Pepys records conflicting evidence: some nights there are disruptions and on others the behaviour is entirely acceptable. Vincent speaks of noisy gallants but a French traveller in 1767 claims 'one never hears any noise'. With the coming of actresses to the stage more women seemingly attended the playhouse and whilst some of these were prostitutes who took up their position in the galleries, others in the 1680s lobbied for the presentation of tragedy and humane comedy.[4]

Restoration dramatists and the repertoire

One must not forget that the arrival of Charles from the continent brought with it an interest in French plays and the acceptance of French actresses. During the reign of his father, when a similar troupe appeared they were driven from the stage, accused of being 'hussies'.

Molière

There was a growing interest in the works of French playwrights, one of whom was Molière, whose work is often performed in translation today. The continental Jesuit schools were renowned for their dramatic performances and the young Molière whilst studying at one of these may have taken part in them. On leaving school Molière formed a strong friendship with a family of actors named Béjart. At the age of 21 he left home, becoming a member of the Béjart troupe, performing in an indoor tennis court in Paris which became known as L'Illustre-Theatre. The actors soon shared premises with a company of *commedia dell'arte* performers managed by Tiberio Fiorillo known as Scaramouche. Commedia companies often relied on a conventional scene of houses arranged around a square (*The Comedy of Errors* by Shakespeare is sometimes produced in a like simultaneous setting) but this was limiting and larger premises were sought at the Palais-Royal. Here Molière and his company stayed until the writer's death fifteen years later.

This was a busy time for Molière as he wrote with speed plays such as *Le Misanthrope* (1666), *Le Bourgeois Gentilhomme* (1660) and *Le Malade Imaginaire* (1673). In 1664 *Don Juan* appeared, a theme which became popular in England with the presentation of Thomas Shadwell's play *The Libertine* (1675); Juan later appeared in the context of a serious ballet with music and songs by William Reeve. The Don is a man possessed by curiosity, brought to the notice of the audience by the list of questions he asks Sgnarelle as soon as he makes his first appearance. But Don Juan uses language primarily as a weapon of defence and contact through the word has a secondary place. Christopher Hampton has written of him: 'Words are meaningless because they do not touch his body' – for him physicality only exists in his lust and in those physical barriers such as the storm, the capsized boat, his pursuers, that prevent him achieving his objectives – and finally his eternal punishment is represented on stage in terms of physical burning as he sinks crashing into hell.[5]

Drama in England

The principal ingredients of the repertoire in England during the Restoration period may be grouped as:

- heroic drama
- the rediscovery of Shakespeare
- opera and spectacle
- Restoration comedy.

English heroic drama

One gains a picture of English heroic drama from George Villier's (Duke of Buckingham) burlesque *The Rehearsal* (1671), even though this is a satire. We must remember that the form and conventions of heroic drama were imported to England from France: this is classical tragedy on the theme of 'love and honour', written in rhymed couplets in which the unities of time (the plot usually ran its course within the span of a day), place (the location of the plot was usually restricted to a single place; obviously Shakespeare with his transfers throughout the Roman and Egyptian world in *Anthony and Cleopatra* does not maintain a unity of place) and action (normally reported rather than enacted on the stage in view of the spectator as with the death of Jocasta in *Oedipus Rex*). The form Villiers uses was of the play within a play with the central character, Bayes, as the author of the interlude. The audience meets him talking to two acquaintances, Smith and Johnson, the spectators' surrogates, before the rehearsal begins after which three of the actors discuss the projected production. Thus Villiers is able to use two devices almost simultaneously. One of the prime episodes within the play is when Prince Prettiman soliloquises over his boots, the one symbolising honour and the other love, reaching its apogee in the enactment of the stage direction, *Goes out hopping with one boot on, and the other off*. The author had been so long in the writing that at times it is difficult to deduce exactly who is lampooned: however it is generally accepted that Villiers's target is the dramatist and Poet Laureate John Dryden and the play *The Conquest of Granada* (1670).

Dryden's play *The Indian Emperor or the Conquest of Mexico by the Spaniards* (1665) is particularly useful for our purposes as William Hogarth painted a performance of the play given by child actors at the Great George Street home of John Conduitt, the Master of the Mint. First the play: the historical point reached is the arrival in Mexico of Cortés, the Spanish conqueror and explorer. The audience meets Montezuma in a careworn middle age and Pizarro, the title role of the future drama by Richard Sheridan. One of the memorable points in a long and to some extent loosely connected series of plots is in the final act in which Montezuma is tortured on a rack whilst a Spanish priest and Pizarro conduct a dialogue with him sizing up the relative merits of revealed and natural religion. Instead of this debate pulling the drama together, one is aware of a strong element of black comedy and a condemnation of Spanish Catholicism. Second, Hogarth's painting: for the artist's purposes the focus is on the audience, a series of portraits enlivened by chatter and a dropped fan; one may learn of several theatre practices from the *ad hoc* performance space shown. A platform has been erected above which, in order to light the actors principally rather than the scenes, two hoops of candles are visible. The way in which shadows are cast partly indicate that there may also have been side lighting from at least one of the wings. A wooden beam provides a proscenium arch and a swagged curtain appears to hang from this. The scenery, presumably representing the prison, stands immediately at the rear of the acting area. Some light seen through a grating suggests that the scenic area, as in a purpose-built theatre, continues further upstage. Shallow wing pieces, possibly of unpainted fabric, hang at the sides of the stage. A child performer speaks directly to the audience and three others are seen in part-profile listening to her. Theophilus Cibber, manager of Drury Lane, helped to coach the children in their roles; he may also have had a hand in designing the scenery.

Thomas Otway's play *Venice Preserv'd* was first seen in 1682, shafted with plot and counter-plot, the atmosphere that Englishmen breathed at this time. Three years earlier Titus Oates had fabricated a rumour that the Pope was supporting a plot to murder Charles II and so restore the Catholic faith in England to establish military control of the country. But this is background material: Otway's source was a fictional work by the Abbé de Sainte-Real centring on a conspiracy of the Spaniards against the Republic of Venice in 1618. In the play the central character at the time of the early performances was Jaffeir, played by the actor Betterton and later Quin but thereafter the great tragic actors, such as J P Kemble and Charles William Macready, played Pierre, suggesting that the audience had shifted the interpretation of the play. The third of the triumvirate at the heart of the drama was Belvidera, originally played by Elizabeth Barry. To condense the plot into a couple of sentences reduces Otway's work to a melodrama, but this is a common danger. Belvidera's father, Priuli, orders her to be unhoused, incensed that her husband is not bringing money into the family and treats Jaffeir, the husband, with harshness, so giving Jaffeir an opportunity to revenge his loss of dignity; Jaffeir joins a conspiracy, agreeing to put up Belvidera as a hostage, but she later persuades her husband to betray the plotters, including Pierre, his friend. The heroic thread is strengthened when Pierre confuses personal injury with universal justice and Jaffeir is shown as a man caught between wicked revolutionaries and a vicious senate. Is Jaffeir an over-susceptible man of sensibility? Possibly, but one contrasts him, protecting Pierre against shame and torture, with Belvidera, who

THE COMMONWEALTH AND RESTORATION STAGE   75

goes mad, unable to endure the sins of her husband and her own emotions, finding in Jaffeir the stability of heroic tragedy. This is a play to be seen rather than read; it is occasionally performed but difficult to come by.

The rediscovery of Shakespeare

Many playwrights looked to the dramatists of the past for their plots: Beaumont and Fletcher could serve with a minimum of adaptation but Molière was both stimulus and quarry; Shakespeare seemed at times uncouth and at others pessimistic so that rectifications were made. Nahum Tate, Poet Laureate, adapted *King Lear* with many of the characters continuing in an off-stage existence such as Cordelia and Edgar, happily married, and Lear in his contented dotage. Popular taste dictated that the Fool had become superfluous and he was omitted. John Dryden rewrote *Antony and Cleopatra* bringing it within the confines of the dramatic unities under the title *All for Love* (1678). Two of the comedies which offered material for filleting and a presentation by children, *The Tempest* and *A Midsummer Night's Dream* are examples of the use to which original material was put. Later Garrick was to present *The Taming of the Shrew* as a cut-down afterpiece renamed *Katherine and Petruchio* (1756).

Opera and spectacle

In 1685 John Dryden defined opera as 'a poetical Tale... represented by Vocal and Instrumental Musick, adorned with Scenes, machines, and Dancing'.[6] Obviously, the visual aspects were as important, at least in the expectation, as the musical and dramatic. Sir William Davenant had established a vogue for opera before the return of Charles with such pieces as *The Cruelty of the Spaniards in Peru* (1658) in which Dryden's subsequent definition was to be found. An example of a Dryden opera is *King Arthur* (1691) with music by Henry Purcell, a success that held the stage until the 1840s. In the dedicatory epistle Dryden conceded that the music was pre-eminent: '...the Numbers of Poetry and Vocal Musick are sometimes so contrary, that in many Places I have been oblig'd to cramp my Verses, and make them rugged to the Reader, that they may be harmonious to the Hearer'. *King Arthur* he called a 'dramatic opera', thus differentiating it from an 'Italian opera'. In the former the dialogue is spoken whilst in the latter speaking was restricted solely to interludes with comic characters and recitative replaced speech. A brief, simplified opera, *Dido and Aeneas* (1689), that Nahum Tate wrote for a girls' school – again with music by Purcell – is well worth hearing. It was eventually brought from school to stage but unfortunately set as an interlude in an adaptation of *Measure for Measure* (1700) by Charles Gildon. The plot, based on episodes in *The Aeneid* by Virgil, is a retelling of the story of Dido falling in love with Aeneas when he is shipwrecked on the Carthaginian coast. Ordered by the gods, Aeneas forsakes her and Dido kills herself.

Entertainments in the theatre refuse to allow themselves to be imprisoned within time capsules. John Gay's ballad opera, *The Beggar's Opera*, very conveniently follows on here although the date of the first production, 1728, suggests it should figure in the following chapter. The entertainment was initially a great success and the audience approved the rash unconventionality of the work:

On Monday was represented for the first time [wrote a critic in the *Daily Journal*, 1 February 1728] at the Theatre Royal in Lincoln's Inn Fields, Mr Gay's new English opera, written in a manner wholly new, and very entertaining, there being introduced, instead of Italian airs, above 60 of the most celebrated English and Scotch tunes. There was present then, as well as last night, a prodigious concourse of nobility and gentry, and no theatrical performance for these many years has met with so much applause.

It was quickly alleged that Gay had three objectives in writing the piece: this was a vehicle by which Italian opera was ridiculed; Sir Robert Walpole and his Whig government were reputed to have been attacked in the piece; the *modus vivendi* of whores and criminals appeared to be glorified. Dean Swift declared in the *Intelligencer* (25 May 1728) that the presentation had exposed 'the unnatural taste for Italian music among [the English] which is totally unsuitable to our northern climate, and the genius of the people, whereby we are overrun with Italian effeminacy and Italian nonsense'. He went on to claim that an elderly gentleman some years previous had remarked when 'the practice of an unnatural vice grew frequent in London', that this would be the forerunner of Italian operas and singers. Barbs supposedly fired at Walpole are difficult to substantiate. However, a reference to Bob Booty (1.2) allegedly referred to the first minister and a quarrel episode between Peachum and Lockit (2.10), Macklin reported in his *Memoirs*, alluded to an argument between Sir Robert and Lord Townshend.[7] Walpole's *ménage a trois* with his wife and Maria Skerrett, his mistress, was picked up by Lord Hervey in Macheath's incarceration in prison when he was confronted by his two 'wives'.[8] Gay's model for Peachum seems to have been Jonathan Wild the highwayman with details taken from Henry Fielding's novel.[9]

Restoration comedy

The popularity of Restoration comedy has outweighed other forms of the period and here there is room only to look at several representative works; however the book lists in

sections two and three of this chapter are a guide to
widening one's knowledge.

William Wycherley: *The Country Wife*

As Sheridan did one hundred years later in *The School for
Scandal* (1777), Wycherley in *The Country Wife* (1675)
paints a picture of life in London, the area off Covent Garden
Piazza. He works on three levels. There is the plot
concerned with Horner, the cuckolder of husbands, who
claims that he has become impotent because of a sexual
disease, so opening the way to many affairs. There is the
coming to town of Margery, the country wife of the title, not
a bumpkin as she is sometimes shown but the sister of a titled
sibling from the Hampshire 'placehouse' or estate of an
aristocrat, for her marriage to Pinchwife, an experienced
lecher. And there is the genuine romantic interest of Frank
Harcourt and Alithea, possibly the only marriage in the play
one would be prepared to back. After the early
performances at Drury Lane the play was found offensive.
Certainly there is a strong sexual interest running
throughout: Horner's very name refers to the horns a
cuckold (a man whose wife has been seduced by another)
is often depicted wearing and when Margery visits the New
Exchange (3.2) she is amazed by the shop and inn signs
hanging outside the buildings, – the Bull's Head, the Ram's
Head and the Stag's Head, all horned creatures like the
cuckold. This sniffing out of sexuality reaches its height in
Horner's lodgings (4.3), to which Lady Fidget has gone after
telling her husband she is visiting a china house; china was
the sign of fragile virginity but in this scene a mention of
china suggests copulation for, as Lady Fidget says, Horner
'knows china very well, and has himself very good, but will
not let me see it lest I should beg some'. In addition to this
strong sexual bias, Wycherley explores through his
characters current attitudes towards women, the townsman's

attitude towards the country and, finally, the deception rife in the town and this includes disguise. Horner, for example, takes the role of domestic chaplain to Sparkish and this allows the twin themes of copulation and disguise to meet: Lucy makes an aside to Alithea that Parson Horner will preach in her pulpit, a euphemism for intercourse. This bold knowing shocked many in the audience and it was left to David Garrick to reframe Wycherley's text, turning it into a milksop afterpiece, *The Country Girl* (1766) with Dorothy Jordan often playing the title role.

John Vanbrugh, *The Relapse* and John Crowne, *Sir Courtly Nice*

Both John Vanbrugh and John Crowne developed their own macaronic characters; Sir Novelty Fashion who progressed up the social hierarchy to become Lord Foppington, appearing in *The Relapse* (1696), was the creation of Vanbrugh and Crowne created Sir Courtly Nice, naming his play (1685) after him. Both men were based on the camp image of the macaroni in exotic clothes, with cane and sometimes mirror in hand and a wig of piled hair; they held the stage until the last part of the eighteenth century in such characters as Sheridan's Sir Benjamin Backbite in *The School for Scandal*. Their speech and the pronunciation of words were affected and the slightest passing of information was wrapped in a badinage of simile and metaphor. Foppington describes his day:

> ...at ten a'clack, I say, I rise. Naw, if I find 'tis a good day, I resolve to take a turn in the Park, and see the fine women; so huddle on my clothes, and get dressed by one. If it be nasty weather, I take a turn in the chocolate house...from thence I go to dinner at Lackets, where you are so nicely and delicately served, that, stap my vitals, they shall compose you a dish no bigger than a saucer, shall

come to fifty shillings. Between eating my dinner...I spend my time, till I go to the play; where, till nine a-clack, I entertain myself with looking upon the company, and usually dispose of one hour more in leading 'em out.[10]

Both of these fops were played by Colley Cibber, a Drury Lane actor and author whose own life was as exaggerated as those he personated.

Restoration figurehead actors

One often thinks of the Restoration actors as flamboyant people on the stage, waving handkerchiefs and fans, indulging in superfluous moves and speaking in an affected voice. In the latter years of his life Thomas Betterton trained young performers, setting on them his spirit of *gravitas* in tragic acting. Unlike many actors Betterton took rehearsals seriously: he expected the young to arrive with lines learned and to be sober and alert. Stage business – which of the proscenium doors one should enter the stage by, for example – was to be committed to memory as also was a position on the stage. Lesser characters tended to stand downstage and important ones, the more especially if they were performed by a well-known actor, were placed upstage: an obvious generalisation but at the same time a useful one. The habit of muttering one's lines during rehearsals Betterton discouraged, although many prompters (an important theatre official who, in addition to directing some of the rehearsals, kept the prompt book and carefully transcribed details of the production therein) were prepared to put up with it.[11] Betterton's own style of speaking on stage was declamatory, very clear but hardly natural. Nevertheless, there was involvement: when the ghost of King Hamlet appeared in Gertrude's closet Betterton turned 'instantly on the sight of his father's spirit, as pale as his neckcloth, when every article of his body seemed to be affected with a tremor inexpressible...'[12]

James Quin continued in the same vein, continuing the habit of declaiming – in fact he was known as the last of the declaimers – and conservative in the extreme; add to this the fact that he was poorly educated and one is not surprised that he had his limitations and that the freer style of David Garrick became the accepted norm in the metropolis during the later Georgian era. Tobias Smollett described Quin's acting: 'His utterance is a continual sing-song, like the chanting of vespers; and his action resembles that of heaving ballast into the hold of a ship.'[13]

2. SELECTED AUTHORS, PLAYWRIGHTS AND WORKS OF THE RESTORATION PERIOD

Note: Play titles are prefixed by an asterisk.

1658: Oliver Cromwell dies

1660: Charles II enthroned

1660: Samuel Pepys begins his diary

1664: *Don Juan by Molière

1665: *The Indian Emperor by John Dryden

1666: Great Fire of London

1666: *Le Misanthrope by Molière

1667: Paradise Lost by John Milton

1671: *The Rehearsal by George Villiers

1671: *Samson Agonistes by John Milton

1671: *Love in a Wood by William Wycherley

1674: *The Enchanted Island by Thomas Shadwell, *et al*, from William Shakespeare

1675: *The Country Wife by William Wycherley

1675: *The Libertine by Thomas Shadwell

1676: *The Man of Mode by George Etherege

1677: *The Rover by Aphra Behn

1678: The Pilgrim's Progress by John Bunyan

1680: *The History of King Lear by Nahum Tate from
        William Shakespeare

       1685: Death of Charles II and enthronement of James II

1682: *Venice Preserv'd by Thomas Otway

1685: *Sir Courtly Nice by John Crowne

       1689: Enthronement of William and Mary

1693: *The Old Bachelor by William Congreve

1696: *The Relapse by John Vanbrugh

1698: A Short View of the Immorality and Profaneness of the
        English Stage by John Collier

       1702: Death of William III and enthronement of Anne

1706: *The Recruiting Officer by George Farquhar

1711: The Spectator by Joseph Addison and Richard Steele

1712: The Rape of the Lock by Alexander Pope

       1714: Death of Anne

1728: *The Beggar's Opera by John Gay

3. BIBLIOGRAPHY

General works on the Restoration Theatre and Restoration Literature

Bevis, Richard W, *English Drama: Restoration and Eighteenth Century, 1660–1789*. London: Longman, 1988.

Birdsall, Virginia Ogden, *Wild Civility: The English Comic Spirit on the Restoration Stage*. Indiana: Indiana University Press, 1970.

Brown, J R, and Harris, B A, eds., *Restoration Theatre*. Stratford upon Avon Studies 6. 1965.

Dobrée, Bonamy, *Restoration Comedy*. 1924.

Dyson, H V D and Butt, John, *Augustans and Romantics, 1689–1830*. London: Cresset Press, 1961.

Fiske, R, *English Theatre Music in the Eighteenth Century*. London: Oxford University Press,1973.

Fitzgerald, Percy, *A New History of the English Stage*. London: Tinsley Brothers, 1882.

Loftis, J, *Comedy and Society from Congreve to Fielding*. Stanford, Calif: Stanford University Press,1959.

McKeon, M, *The Origins of the English Novel, 1600–1740*. London: Radius, 1988.

Milhouse, Judith and Hume, Robert D, *Producible Interpretation*. Carbondale: Southern Illinois University Press, 1985.

Powell, Jocelyn, *Restoration Theatre Production*. London: Routledge, 1984.

Ranger, Paul, *The Restoration to the Romantics*. London: LAMDA Publications, 1996.

Smith, D F, *The Critics in the Audiences of the London Theatres from Buckingham to Sheridan*. Albuquerque, New Mexico: 1953.

Spencer, Hazelton, *Shakespeare Improved*. Cambridge, Mass: Harvard University Press, 1927.

Wilson, J H, 'Rant, Cant and Tone on the Restoration Stage', in *Studies in Philology*, 52 (1955), pp. 592–8.

Staging

Hotson, Leslie, *The Commonwealth and Restoration Stage*. New York: Russell and Russell, 1962.

Summers, Montague, *The Playhouse of Pepys*. London: Routledge, 1935.

Biography

Wilson, J H, *All the King's Ladies*. Chicago: University of Chicago Press, 1958.

Betterton, Thomas

Gildon, Charles, *The Life of Mr Thomas Betterton*. London: 1710.

Cibber, Colley

Cibber Colley, *An Apology for His Life*. London: Everyman, 1938.

Dryden, John

Fujimura, Thomas H, *The Temper of John Dryden*. East Lansing, Mich: Colleagues Press, 1998.

Gay, John

Irving, W H, *John Gay: Favourite of the Wits*. Durham, North Carolina: Duke University Press, 1940.

Vanbrugh, John

Bingham, M, *Masks and Facades: Sir John Vanbrugh*. London: Allen and Unwin,1974.

Villiers, George

Wilson, J H, *A Rake and His Times*. New York: 1954.

Wycherley, William

McCarthy, B Eugene, *William Wycherley: A Biography*. [Athens]: Ohio University Press, 1979.

Iconography

The following three books are a valuable source of illustrations of the Restoration theatre:

Craik, T W, ed., *The Revels History of Drama in English. Volume V, 1660–1750*. London: Methuen and Co Ltd, 1976.

Hartnoll, Phyllis, *The Theatre: A Concise History*. London: Thames and Hudson, reprinted 1995.

Thomas, David, ed., *Restoration and Georgian England, 1660–1788*. Cambridge: Cambridge University Press, 1989.

For theatrical portraits of this and other periods see:

Kerslake, J F, ed, *Catalogue of Theatrical Portraits in London Public Collections*. London: Society for Theatre Research, 1961.

Critical writings on some of the works listed in section two

Addison, Joseph

Lewis, C S, 'Addison' in *Essays on the Eighteenth Century Presented to David Nicol Smith*. Oxford: Clarendon Press, 1945.

Crowne, John

McMullin, B J, ed., *The Comedies of John Crowne: A Critical Edition*. New York: 1984.

Davenant, William

Bordinat, P and Blaydes, S B, *Sir William Davenant*. New York: Garland, 1986.

Dryden, John

Myers, W G, *Dryden*. London: Hutchinson University Library, 1973.

Gay, John

Gay, John, *The Beggar's Opera*, ed. Brian Loughfrey and T O Treadwell. Harmondsworth: Penguin Books, 1986.

Nokes, David, *John Gay. A Profession of Friendship*. Oxford: Oxford University Press, 1995.

Otway, Thomas

Taylor, A M, *Next to Shakespeare*. Durham, North Carolina: Duke University Press, 1950.

Waith, E M, 'Tears of magnanimity in Otway and Racine' in *French and English Drama of the Seventeenth Century*. Los Angeles: William Andrews Clark Memorial Library, 1972.

Vanbrugh, John

Berkowitz, G M, *Sir John Vanbrugh and the End of Restoration Comedy*. Amsterdam: Rodopi, 1981.

Harris, B A, *Sir John Vanbrugh*. Writers and their Work, no. 197. London: Longmans, 1967.

Villiers, George

O'Neill, J H, *George Villiers, Second Duke of Buckingham*. Boston, Mass: Twayne, 1984.

Wycherley, William

Neill, Michael, 'Horned Beasts and China Oranges: Reading the signs in *The Country Wife*', *Eighteenth-Century Life*, 12 (1988), pp. 3–17.

Thompson, J, *Language in Wycherley's Plays*. Alabama: University of Alabama Press, 1984.

Zimbado, R A, *Wycherley's Drama*. New Haven and London: Yale University Press, 1965.

4. DISCUSSION POINTS

* Outline the development of the theatre from its Elizabethan structure to the end of the Restoration period.

* Is Horner (*The Country Wife*) the hero or the villain of the piece?

* 'A new appreciation of the countryside blossomed with the return of a monarchical court.' Can you justify this statement from poems of the period you have read?

* To what extent are primary source materials (contemporary portraits of performers, engravings of contemporary theatre buildings, journal accounts of performances seen immediately prior to writing, playbills issued at the time of a performance, etc) useful in the study of theatre history?

* Is the principal character in a novel of this period different in kind to one in a play?

* Which writer of the Restoration period did you find the most interesting to read (or if a dramatist, to see his/her work)?

5. NOTES AND REFERENCES

1   A sectional drawing of the theatre ascribed to Wren is housed at All Souls College, Oxford.

2   T W Craik, ed., *The Revels History of Drama in English, vol V, 1660–1750*. London: Methuen and Co Ltd, 1976, p. 85.

3   The components are given by John Dryden in a prologue to *Marriage a la Mode* (1762); see John Dryden, *Poems*, ed. James Kinsley. Oxford: Clarendon Press, 1958, 1. 145.

4   The examples given here are cited by Richard W Bevis in *English Drama: Restoration and Eighteenth Century, 1660–1789*. London and New York: Longman, 1988, pp 31–2.

5   Molière, *Don Juan*, translated by Christopher Hampton. London: Faber and Faber, 1974, pp. 15–20.

6   The definition appears in the preface to Dryden's *Albion and Albanius*.

7   [William Cooke], *The Memoirs of Charles Macklin*. London: James Asperne, 1804, p. 54.

8   John Hervey, *Memoirs of the Reign of George the Second*, ed. J W Croker. London: Bickers and Son, 1884, 1. iii; 1. 15n.

9   Henry Fielding, *The Life of Jonathan Wild the Great*, 1743.

10 John Vanbrugh, *The Relapse*. London: 1697, Act 2, scene 1.

11 This section is based on Charles Gildon, *The Life of Mr Thomas Betterton*. London: 1710, p. 15.

12 *The Laureat or The Right Side of Colley Cibber, Esq.* London: 1740.

13 Tobias Smollett, *Peregrine Pickle*, ed. J L Clifford. London, New York, Toronto: Oxford University Press, 1964, pp. 274.

THE GEORGIAN STAGE AND CONTINENTAL INFLUENCES

1.   SURVEY

The social context

The accession in England in 1714 of George I of the House
of Hanover provides a starting point to the Georgian period
and continues until the death of William IV in 1837. Two acts
of parliament had a bearing on the fortunes of the Georgian
stage. The first, in 1737, originated in Sir Robert Walpole's
discovery that the manager of the Little Theatre in the
Haymarket, Samuel Foote, had lampooned his cabinet. The
First Minister decreed that only those theatres which had
been granted a royal patent – the Theatres Royal in Drury
Lane and Covent Garden together with a few theatres in
towns of royal residence such as York, Brighton and
Richmond-upon-Thames – were to be allowed to present
entertainments: the remainder were closed. The law was
often breached, especially by managers who advertised a
'Concert of Music' with the presentation of dramatic pieces
gratis between the selections to the extent that the
prohibition became ridiculous, prompting in 1788 a further
act which allowed non-patent theatres to present plays for
a run of up to sixty nights. It was then time for the company
to move on to another playhouse and the count began again.
Thus managers, whether they worked in the metropolis or
the provinces, tended to lease or buy a number of theatres
within easy travelling distance of each other and to move
around the circuit, timing their arrival to coincide with events
such as fairs or horse-races. An example is Thomas Collins,
a Wiltshire man, whose principal theatres lay in the towns of
Salisbury, Southampton, Winchester, Portsmouth and
Chichester.

The design of the Georgian theatre

The London Georgian theatre is an extension of the design of the Restoration theatre. The audience was still seated in the three areas of box, pit and gallery which together formed the auditorium; into this space the acting area of the stage jutted, flanked on either side by a proscenium door through which the majority of the entrances and exits were made. Rows of boxes continued on to the sides of the acting space, too.

An inner stage formed the scenic area divided from the front stage by the proscenium arch and immediately behind this hung the green proscenium curtain, normally raised at the start of the play until the epilogue was to be spoken 'before the curtain' by one of the characters. The back scene was painted on a pair of shutters that ran in grooves so that, when there was to be a change of location, stagehands could pull the shutters apart, revealing the next stage picture. To give a sense of perspective, five sets of grooves held the wing pieces and these could be similarly altered by stagehands. The inner stage was lit by rows of candles or lamps standing at the base or the sides of the wing pieces. There might also be banks of candles standing in the wings backed by coloured silks which gave a particular tint to the lighting – such as blue to suggest moonlight – and were capable of being quickly substituted for another colour. The actors on the forestage also required to be lit. At the beginning of the Georgian period chandeliers hung from the ceiling above the area but later oil lamps (Argands) were arranged at the front of the stage to form footlights; these could be lowered when it was desired to darken the area.

At mid-century the theatres were intimate buildings but by the end of the eighteenth century so great was the demand to see performers of quality that great barns of theatres were constructed, calling from the actors magnificent projection and exaggerated postures.

Provincial theatres

In the 1730s and 40s groups of actors were to be found travelling on carts making their way from a barn or tavern out-building in one village to another: these make-shift playhouses are often difficult to track down as they are referred to in playbills simply as 'The Theatre'. In towns, places of greater refinement were often used such as town halls, market houses and indoor tennis courts. The passing of the 1788 Theatres Act gave managers a sense of security and they were ready to put up purpose-built playhouses which, when not in use for dramatic presentations, served for lecture halls, dances and one-person shows.

The performers in a provincial company usually consisted of the manager, his wife, possibly the parents of one or the other who would take the older roles, and such siblings and cousins as were available. Sometimes, as with the Cheltenham Company, three generations would provide managers, in this instance the Boles Watsons.

Performance style

The latter half of the eighteenth century is often described as 'the age of the actor'. In our own day naturalism is a highly prized accomplishment but not so in Georgian times; then the aim was to adopt a stance over a number of lines and to declaim the text of the play. When a change of mood was evident, the stance or 'attitude' was altered but usually repose continued to underpin the speaking. In studying engravings of performers, both men and women from roughly 1750 to 1820, it is evident that the spine is stretched upwards and the legs are spaced wide apart with one leg taking the weight of the body: this is evident even beneath a woman's skirt. One hand or the lower part of the arm, normally the left, articulates with the upper body and the right hand is used for gestures, pointing, holding a dagger or any other activity. Henry Siddons compiled a book of illustrations, complete with commentary, on gesture and action demonstrating the posture needed for the portrayal of such emotions as fear, hate, love, patriotism. This is a form of 'shorthand acting'.[1]

Least this should seem over-static it was customary to use occasionally a 'galvanisation' in which the performer suddenly became highly energetic, leaping, for example, from a window embrasure into a castle moat or demonstrating a fit on the stage. In spite of suffering from arthritis in his legs John Philip Kemble was extraordinarily adept at these sudden bursts of furious activity.

Both the attitude and the galvanisation were a means of signalling to the audience and they in turn were prompted either to maintain a deep silence or even to weep with pity (the discovery of the long-lost child by his titled mother in John Home's *Douglas* brought on these silent tears) or to applaud the ferocity of the galvanisation which could aspire to its apogee as the hero sprang from the side of the stage into the wings glancing at the faces of the house as he went. A further method of 'telling the narration', and one completely out of favour at present, was for the members of the cast on stage to stand facing the audience, in a line near to the footlights and in the delivery of speeches to include them. Thus those at the theatre were often participating in the play as if they were a further composite character in the drama.

Performance style does not continue without development and change. Come the beginning of the nineteenth century the acting area was used less frequently. The performers became subsumed into the landscape of the scenic area. One reason for this trend was the growing popularity of 'castle plays' which finished with a grand assault on the villain's fortified lair, thus naturally demanding that the cast played upstage as soldiers rammed the castle gates or scaled the walls. For some plays dungeon settings were required and here again the actors were needed within the confines of the prison area.[2] By the beginning of the 1820s acting itself was less formal and people patently assumed the characters they were playing. Two actors with an interest in what motivates a central character were William Charles Macready and Edmund Kean; the latter specialised in villainous roles such as Macbeth, Othello and Sir Giles Overreach. That Kean had an affair with the wife of a London alderman, Charlotte Cox, and wrote her letters that, according to a judge were 'fiery, fluent and filthy', added to his villainous interest. The lives of actor and role were beginning to merge.

The repertoire

In the Georgian period the repertoire covered a wide range of subjects, so the following remarks are of necessity sketchy. Soon after the mid-eighteenth century there was a flourish of dramas in which the upper echelons of society were scrutinised, not to provoke laughter in the audience, as had been the custom in comedies of the Restoration period, but to elicit sympathy. A work from which many a young 'spouter' knew long passages by heart was the Rev John Home's play *Douglas* (1756), basically the story of the recognition by Lady Randolph of her long-lost son Norval. Other plays showing the tribulations of the upper classes are *The Countess of Salisbury* (1765) by Hall Hartson and *The Grecian Daughter* (1772) by the newspaper editor and critic Arthur Murphy. Perhaps it was the strong influence of Sarah Siddons which decreed that actresses should be given more important roles than heretofore and hence we have *The Heroine of the Cave* (1774) by Paul Hiffernan,

Albina, Countess of Raimond (1779) by Hannah Cowley
and *Julia* (1787) – with her 'polish'd front' and 'blue slender
veins', somewhat common attributes of the heroine of the
period – by Robert Jephson.

Passing mention has been made of the 'castle play' in
which incarceration in the dungeon, murder and the
unmasking of villainy, either by an army or more
wonderfully by a young hero, all featured. Titles of several
of these are: *The Castle of Andalusia* (1782) by John
O'Keeffe, *The Enchanted Castle* (1786) by Miles Peter
Andrews (who also wrote *The Mysteries of the Castle*,
1795) and *The Castle Spectre* (1797) by Matthew Lewis,
then a 22-year-old youth with such talent that Dorothy
Jordan, John Barrymore and John Philip Kemble – who
disliked the play and retaliated in 1812 with *Lodoiska*, a
drama in the same vein – appeared in the first production
at Drury Lane. The convent or monastic building had the
same qualities as the castle: both were removed from
society, guarded by robust canvas walls and complete with
secret passages and dungeons, all accoutrements Lewis
used in his macabre novel *The Monk* (1796). No monastic
community was complete without its tyrannous abbot or
prioress who took over the role of villain: 'You are to
receive three hundred lashes on the back,' the Prior told
Martin – disguised as a novice – in *The Sicilian Romance*
(1794) by Henry Siddons. Experiments in creating convent
churches were a popular pastime for scenic designers. For
Joanna Baillie's play *De Monfort* (1800) at Drury Lane,
William Capon, an enthusiast for mediaeval architecture,
built a vista of arches 52 feet in depth receding to the back
of the scenic area. 'The interior perspective of the
convent,' wrote Thomas Dutton, 'ranks among the
grandest scenes the stage can boast.'[3] The ravages of
time could be combined with disintegrating convent
buildings giving the effect of a Turner landscape: this

occurred in *Fontainville Forest* (1794), a dramatisation by James Boaden of Ann Radcliffe's romance in which Madame Lamotte shelters with her family amongst the crumbling remnants of arches and vaults.

Accurate settings of foreign locations became so popular that plays were placed as far afield as Peru in the case of *Pizarro* (1799) by Richard Brinsley Sheridan, the story of the attempted suppression of the Peruvians by the Spanish conquistadors, or in the fabled lands of Blue Beard's kingdom in the play of that name (1798) by George Colman the Younger. Beyond the desire for scenic marvels, the new century brought a wish for further excitement and spectacle which could only be satisfied by Kemble in his provision of two interludes in his revival of *Blue Beard*: in each of these a troupe of horses provided by Astley's Amphitheatre galloped onto the stage to attack Blue Beard's flimsy pier-like construction, expiring when they were shot into the moat 'as gracefully...as the English tragedians', remarked an American tourist.[4]

However, it was a setting on home ground that provided Sheridan's comedies and a single play by Oliver Goldsmith with lasting fame. The city of Bath with its piazza and elegant streets was the backdrop for *The Rivals* (1775) and Mayfair gave a home to *The School for Scandal* (1777) revealing a number of interiors in which Sheridan had an interest as, newly wed, he was attempting to buy a house in the neighbourhood. In contrast an anonymous countryside of ponds, hills, taverns and lanes surrounded the Hardcastle's rambling home, giving Dorothy Hardcastle the fright of her life in the last act of *She Stoops to Conquer* (1773).

Percy Fitzgerald remembered as a young lad that the best plays ended with a grand 'blow-up', especially when the stage had been peopled with banditti, gypsies and a well-tanned hero. *The Miller and his Men* (1813) by

Isaac Pocock provided this spectacle admirably. Grindoff, miller by day and captain of the banditti by night, lived at the flour-mill which Ravina mined and exploded. Smoke and magnesium flashes partly hid the mechanics of the scene: ropes heaved at wedges of masonry that flew from the walls, the stage manager catapulted life size dolls into the air, the orchestra played and the lair of the banditti came tumbling down. This was the stuff of Georgian theatre.

The performers

The eighteenth century was known as 'the age of the actor' and so numerous were they and so diverse their talents that one can mention only a few. David Garrick was an all-round man of the theatre. He is remembered for two objectives. The first was the simplification of the performers' acting. Prior to his management of Drury Lane the exaggerated gestures and speech of the Restoration stage prevailed but Garrick attempted to instil into the company a naturalness of speech and gesture. Secondly he worked to make the production a unity in which costumes were planned to correspond with the scenes and lighting and to this end he employed Philippe Jacques de Loutherbourg, an artist from Alsace, to oversee the designs and Alexander Johnston to work with him on the elaborate machines used in the mounting of spectacles. The first objective was not totally achieved as some of the younger members of the Kemble family adopted the statuesque poses, often admired by the audience.

Virtually all of this family was engaged in the theatre. Roger, the paterfamilias who managed a touring company in the west Midlands, had hoped that his son John Philip would study for the priesthood at Douai Abbey but this was not to be. Charles Kemble, as well as acting, was co-manager of Covent Garden; Stephen was born in the wings of the Hereford Theatre and later in life enjoyed a girth that enabled him to play Falstaff without padding; Sarah, named after her mother, married into the Siddons family and became one of the most famous tragic heroines the English stage has known. A splendidly dignified portrait of her as 'Melpomene, the Tragic Muse' was painted by Sir Joshua Reynolds; numbers of other portraits of her were the work of Sir Thomas Lawrence.

One could almost include Charles Frederick Cooke amongst the Kembles for he adopted the same manner of freezing an emotion into a pose. Indeed Kemble, Siddons and Cooke were known as the 'tragic triumvirate'. Unfortunately Cooke was an alcoholic, frequently unable to appear. Yet he was punctilious in his apology to the audience when he could take to the stage again: 'The old trouble,' he would explain.

Garrick's work also tended to be undone by Sheridan who succeeded to the management. He favoured stylised speaking. A *bête noir* was Dorothy Jordan whose informal lyrical speech as Cora in *Pizarro* annoyed him; during rehearsals Sheridan would sit in a stage box beating on the ledge the rhythmic stresses even of prose speeches and expecting Jordan to adhere to this. A number of women in the company, Jordan included, although stemming from humble beginnings, became aristocratic ladies. Dorothy Jordan was the mistress of the Duke of Clarence (later William IV) living at Bushy Park in Middlesex. Mrs Abington, from humble beginnings as a milliner's assistant, became the mistress of the member of Parliament for Newry and as such was able to guide other actresses in matters of etiquette and speaking; she made her mark as the first Lady Teazle in *The School for Scandal*. Elizabeth Farren, the child of strolling players, became the wife of the Earl of Derby; her tall figure and natural grace aided her portrayal of heroines such as the first Kate

Hardcastle in *She Stoops to Conquer*.

The increasing realism of scenery, the scaling down of the size of London theatres as the nineteenth century progressed and changes of taste helped to ensure that acting became natural and unaffected. By the time the front of the pit had given way to orchestral stalls acting had moved behind the proscenium arch and was surrounded by scenery suggesting a complete room, ceiling included, and only the fourth wall missing. Actors began to perform as if they were in the confines of a drawing room, addressing each other rather than playing to the front of the stage.

The audience

At the beginning of the Georgian period such London citizens as 'Peers, Poets, Nabobs, Jews and Prentice Beaux' – the words are those of the playwright Miles Peter Andrews – tended to sit in the boxes, the most expensive seats.[5] However, a downward social curve gradually brought wealthier trades-people into that region of the auditorium. Some titled people could be found in the pit alongside lawyers of the Inns of Court together with other professional people, not forgetting writers and critics among whom were numbered William Hazlitt and Leigh Hunt. Labouring classes would climb up into the first and second, or topmost, gallery.

The patent theatres in London from about 1750 charged five shillings for a box seat facing the stage, three shillings for a seat in the pit and one or two shillings for the two galleries. There were also side boxes but these were 'few in number, and very incommodious' according to the Earl of Carlisle.[6] Half price was charged for admittance after the end of the third act of the main piece.

Much the same divisions of society were to be found in the country theatres although here the prices were cheaper, usually three shillings (boxes), two shillings (pit) and one shilling (gallery). Half price was also offered at the country theatres. It must be remembered that although seats were cheaper than in London many of the provincial playhouses were adaptations of other buildings and not particularly comfortable.

German theatre in the eighteenth century

Drama developed late in Germany. For several hundred years the stock fare had been improvised harlequinades sometimes combined with violent events in high places; it was time that the literary work of the dramatist took over. The influence of Shakespeare's plays was felt and bourgeois dramas together with sentimental comedies stemmed from France. 'Sturm und Drang', storm and stress, was an aspect of eighteenth-century German Romanticism which pervaded many works: it spoke of the doctrine of the rights of man and advocated, as had Rousseau, a return to the simplicity of nature.

Johann Wolfgang von Goethe, a prolific poet, novelist of stature and dramatist, was director of the Weimar Court Theatre and later of the National Theatre in Berlin. The Shakespeare influence is evident in his play *Berlichingen mit der eisernen Hand* (1773) in which a heroic young man becomes worn down by the degeneracy of the times; it was later Englished by Sir Walter Scott. In 1787 he took Euripides's tragedy, *Iphigenia among the Taurians* – the story of Iphigenia who serves as a priestess of Artemis in the land of the Taurians and there learns that she is to sacrifice her brother on the coming of the Greeks – and presented it under the title *Iphigenie auf Tauris* (1787). Alongside this work for sixty years Goethe was fascinated by the legend of Faust which he had first witnessed as a puppet play and which he dramatised intermittently, presenting it in 1808.

During his lifetime Goethe was overshadowed by Friedrich von Schiller. The earliest of his plays, written when he was 22, was *Die Rauber* (*The Robbers*, 1781), a drama with close affinities to the *Sturm und Drang* ethos. In it two brothers adore one woman. An English version was made by Joseph Holman but John Larpent, the Reader of Plays who acted as censor of any to be presented publicly, took exception to the delineation of the brigands as heroic characters; the adaptor was forced to change the principal roles from banditti to Knights Templars in consequence of which the play was renamed *The Red Cross Knights* (1799). Schiller had a professional interest in history and on becoming professor at Jena he made dramatisations of incidents in the lives of such characters as Mary Stuart (1800) and William Tell (1804). The former play, based on an imagined meeting of Elizabeth I and her prisoner queen, enjoys occasional revivals today. As a poet his 'Ode to Joy' is remembered as the work from which Beethoven selected extracts to set to music in his Ninth Symphony.

The third of this trio, August von Kotzebue, was a most prolific writer of melodramas through which runs a broad seam of sentiment. His most successful work was *Menschenhaft und Reue*, the tale of an erring wife who earns the gift (the paradox is purposeful) of forgiveness from her husband through her life of atonement. In England the text was translated by Benjamin Thompson as *The Stranger*, a play which 'wrings every situation of its tear' and staged at Drury Lane in 1798. The role of Mrs Haller, the heroine, was played by Sarah Siddons, appearing opposite her brother John Philip Kemble. A further success of Kotzebue was *Die Spanier in Peru* (1798), translated by Sheridan and staged also at Drury Lane the following year.

The theatre in France

A period of gloom descended after the death of Molière and it became difficult for French theatre-goers to recognise the talents which were to be met with on the stage. Pierre Carlet de Chamblain de Marivaux suffered from this malaise. He wrote for the actors of the Comedie-Italienne whose interest in the *commedia dell'arte* had recently caused them to seem outmoded. By means of Marivaux's plays which harked back to the commedia tangles they recaptured the interest of their patrons. The general theme of his work is an examination of young people in love, whose difficulties – although sometimes self-inflicted – are universally applicable. His style of writing, often paradoxical, always sensitive, was known as *marivauxdage*, at first an opprobrious term, then one of admiration.

Even though his plays are not revived nowadays either in England or France, mention should be made of Voltaire, a classical playwright and a critic as well as the designer and builder of several theatres including that at Ferney. He regarded Marivaux's plays as idiosyncratic. David Garrick and English audiences owe one debt of gratitude to Voltaire: he was responsible for banishing the audience from sitting on the stage: its members were in the way of the large numbers who formed crowd scenes.

He wrote others, but two plays establish the fame of Pierre-Augustin Caron de Beaumarchais, *Le Barbier de Seville* and *Le Mariage de Figaro*. *Le Barbier* was refused by the Comedie-Italienne: their leading actor had been a hairdresser and in consequence the Comedie-Français gained it, staging the piece in 1775. Figaro rapidly became a spokesman for the resentment felt against French society by the populace. Whilst a single figure is criticised in *Le Barbier*, society as a whole is the target for *Le Mariage*, performed nine years later. Five years after the second play gained an airing the storm of the French Revolution broke. In both plays the character of Figaro owes much to Beaumarchais's life and character; he is the precocious page, the thrice married man and a jack of all trades.

2.   SELECTED AUTHORS, PLAYWRIGHTS AND WORKS OF THE GEORGIAN PERIOD

Note: Play titles are prefixed by an asterisk.

    1714:   George I enthroned

1726:   Gulliver's Travels by Jonathan Swift

    1727:   George II enthroned

1728:   *The Beggar's Opera by John Gay

1731:   *The London Merchant by George Lillo

1733:   An Essay on Man by Alexander Pope

1740:   Pamela by Samuel Richardson

1747:   *The Suspicious Husband by Benjamin Hoadley

1750:   Elegy in a Country Churchyard by Thomas Gray

1755:   The Dictionary by Samuel Johnson

    1755:   The Seven Years War begins

1757:   *Douglas by John Home

    1760:   George III enthroned

1759–67: Tristram Shandy by Laurence Sterne

1762:   *Love in a Village by Isaac Bickerstaff

1765:   The Castle of Otranto by Horace Walpole

1771:   *The West Indian by Richard Cumberlan

1772:   *The Grecian Daughter by Arthur Murphy

1773:   *She Stoops to Conquer by Oliver Goldsmith

1775:   *The Rivals by Richard Brinsley Sheridan

1775:   *Le Barbier de Seville by Pierre Carlet de Chamblain de Beaumarchais

1776: United States Declaration of Independence

1777: *The School for Scandal by Richard Brinsley Sheridan

1778: *The Critic by Richard Brinsley Sheridan

1781: End of the United States War of Independence

1784: *Le Mariage de Figaro by Pierre Carlet de Chamblain de Beaumarchais

1785: Vathek by William Beckford

1787: *Inkle and Yarico by George Colman the Younger

1789: French Revolution and the fall of the Bastille

1789: Songs of Innocence by William Blake

1790: *Menschenhass und Reue by August von Kotzebue

1793: Execution of Louis XVI and Marie Antoinette

1794: End of The Terror in France

1794: The Mysteries of Udolpho by Ann Radcliffe

1796: The Monk by Matthew Gregory Lewis

1797: *The Iron Chest by George Colman the Younger

1798: Lyrical Ballads by William Wordsworth and Samuel Taylor Coleridge

1799: *Pizarro by Richard Brinsley Sheridan

1800: *Maria Stuart by Friedrich von Schiller

1800: *De Monfort by Joanna Baillie

1802: *A Tale of Mystery by Thomas Holcroft

1803: War renewed between England and France

1805: Battle of Trafalgar

1810: The Borough by George Crabbe

1813: Pride and Prejudice by Jane Austen

1813: *Remorse by Samuel Taylor Coleridge

1813: *The Miller and his Men by Isaac Pocock

1815: Battle of Waterloo and Treaty of Vienna

1818: Northanger Abbey by Jane Austen

1818: Frankenstein by Mary Shelley

1820:   The Eve of St Agnes, Isabella and Odes by John Keats

1820:   *The Vampire by J R Planché

    1820:   George IV enthroned

1825:   The Life of an Actor by Pierce Egan

1828:   *Luke the Labourer by John Buckstone

1829:   *Black-Eyed Susan by Douglas Jerrold

    1830:   William IV enthroned

1830:   Rural Rides by William Cobbett

1832:   *Faust, part 2 by Goethe

1836:   Pickwick Papers by Charles Dickens

3.   BIBLIOGRAPHY

General Works on the Georgian Theatre

Bevis, Richard W, *The Laughing Tradition: Stage Comedy in Garrick's Day*. Athens and London: University of Georgia Press, 1980.

Booth, Michael R *et al*, *The Revels History of Drama in English*, vol 6, 1750–1880. London: Methuen and Co Ltd, 1975.

Brewer, John, *The Pleasures of the Imagination*. London: HarperCollins, 1997.

Lynch, James Jeremiah, *Box, Pit and Gallery: Stage and Society in Johnson's London*. Berkeley: University of California Press, 1953.

Mackintosh, Iain and Ashton, Geoffrey, *The Georgian Playhouse*. London: The Arts Council of Great Britain, 1975.

Mander, Raymond and Mitchenson, Joe, *The Artist and the Theatre*. London: Heinemann, 1955.

Nicol, Allardyce, *The Garrick Stage: Theatres and Audiences in the Eighteenth Century*. Manchester: Manchester University Press, 1980.

Sherbo, Arthur, *English Sentimental Drama*. East Lansing: Michigan State University Press, 1957.

Theatres in London and the provinces

Chancellor, E Beresford, *The Annals of Covent Garden and its Neighbourhood*. London: Hutchinson and Co Ltd, 1930.

Field, Moira, *The Lamplit Stage: The Fisher Circuit, 1792–1844*. Norwich: Running Angel, 1985.

Grice, Elizabeth, *Rogues and Vagabonds: Or the Actors' Road to Respectability*. Lavenham: Terence Dalton, 1977.

Staging

Allen, Ralph G, 'Kemble and Capon at Drury Lane' in *Educational Theatre Journal*, vol 23. Columbia, Mo: American Theatre Association, 1971.

Downer, Alan S, 'Players and Painted Stage: Eighteenth-Century Acting' in *Publications of the Modern Language Association of America*, vol 58. Menash, Wis: Modern Language Association, 1943.

Downer, Alan S, 'Players and Painted Stage: Nineteenth-Century Acting' in *Publications of the Modern Langauage Association of America*, vol 61. Menash, Wis: Modern Language Association, 1946.

Joppien, Rudiger, *Philippe Jacques de Loutherbourg, RA, 1740–1812*. London: Greater London Council, 1973.

Joseph, Bertram, *The Tragic Actor*. London: Routlege and Kegan Paul, 1959.

Mander, Raymond and Joe Mitchenson, *A Guide to the Maugham Collection of Theatrical Paintings*. London: Heinemann for the National Theatre, 1980.

Ranger, Paul, *Terror and Pity Reign in Every Breast: Gothic Drama in the London Patent Theatres, 1750–1820*. London: Society for Theatre Research, 1991.

Biography

Cooke, George Frederick

Hare, Arnold, *George Frederick Cooke. The Man and the Actor*. London: Society for Theatre Research, 1980.

Cumberland, Richard

Cumberland, Richard, *Memoirs of Richard Cumberland.* London: Lackington, Allen and Co, 1806.

Garrick, David

McIntyre, Ian, *David Garrick.* London: Allen Lane, 1999.

Jordan, Dorothy

Tomalin, Claire, *Mrs Jordan's Profession.* London: Viking, 1994.

Kemble family

Kelly, Linda, *The Kemble Era.* London: Bodley Head, 1980.

Macready, William Charles

Downer, Alan S, *The Eminent Tragedian: William Charles Macready.* Cambridge, Mass: Harvard University Press, 1966.

Sheridan, Richard

Bingham, Madeleine, *Sheridan: The Trail of a Comet.* London: Allen and Unwin, 1972.

Siddons, Sarah

Manvell, Roger, *Sarah Siddons: Portrait of an Actress.* London: Heinemann, 1976.

Critical Works on Some of the Dramatists listed in Section 2

Baillie, Joanna

Carhart, Margaret S, *The Life and Work of Joanna Baillie.* London: Yale University Press, 1923.

Coleridge, Samuel Taylor

Fruman, Norman, *Coleridge, the Damaged Archangel.* London: Allen and Unwin, 1972.

Garrick, David

Burnim, Kalman A, *David Garrick, Director.* Pittsburg: University of Pittsburg Press, 1961.

Goldsmith, Oliver

Ginger, John, *The Notable Man: The Life and Times of Oliver Goldsmith.* London: Hamilton, 1977.

Jeffares, A Norman, *Oliver Goldsmith.* London: Longman Group for the British Council, 1959.

Home, John

Gipson, Alice Edna, *John Home. A Study of his Life and Works.* Caldwell, Idaho: Caxton Printers, 1916.

Jerrold, Douglas

Emeljanov, Victor, *Victorian Popular Dramatists.* Boston, Mass: Twayne, 1987.

Lewis, Matthew Gregory

Summers, Montague, *The Gothic Quest.* London: Fortune Press, rep 1968.

Murphy, Arthur

Dunbar, H H, *The Dramatic Career of Arthur Murphy.* New York: Oxford University Press, 1946.

Richardson, Samuel

Myer, V G, ed., *Samuel Richardson: Passion and Prudence.* London: Vision, 1986.

Sheridan, Richard Brinsley

Donohue, J W, *Dramatic Character in the English Romantic Age.* Princeton: Princeton University Press, 1970.

Loftis, J, *Sheridan and the Drama of Georgian England.* Oxford: Basil Blackwell, 1976.

Sterne, Laurence

De Porte, M V, *Nightmare and Hobbyhorses: Swift, Sterne and Augustan Ideas of Madness.* San Marino, California: 1874.

4.   DISCUSSION POINTS

- Give examples of the portrayal of the supernatural in Georgian literature.

- To what extent does the audience disposition in the theatre reflect social divisions in society?

- How are the various technical elements of a Georgian production fused together? Who do

- you feel is mostly responsible for the harmonisation?
- Does the setting of a play or novel have an effect on the plot and the characters and on the audience's (or reader's) response?
- Who are some of the stock characters one might expect to find on the Georgian stage (or in a novel) in England and the Continent?
- Name – and enlarge on – several social and political events that are reflected directly or indirectly in writings of the period.

5.   NOTES AND REFERENCES

1   Henry Siddons, *Practical Illustrations of Rhetorical Gesture and Action*. Cambridge, Mass: Sherwood, Neely and Jones, 2nd edition improved, 1822.

2   Amongst the many 'dungeon plays' written at this time may be mentioned *The Castle Spectre* (Matthew Lewis), *Adelmorn the Outlaw* (Matthew Lewis), *Feudal Times* (George Colman the Younger) and *Almeyda, Queen of Granada* (Sophia Lee).

3   Thomas Dutton, *The Dramatic Censor*. London: J Bell, 2. 133.

4   Louis Simond, *An American in Regency England*, ed. Christopher Hibbert (1968), p. 130.

5   Andrews's prologue to *The Dramatist* by Frederick Reynolds, first performed at the Theatre Royal Covent Garden, 1789.

6   The Earl of Carlisle, *Thoughts upon the Present Condition of the Stage*, 1809 cited in Watson Nicholson, *The Struggle for a Free Stage in London*. New York, 1966, pp. 182–3.

THE NINETEENTH CENTURY: PLAYS, POETRY AND NOVELS

1. SURVEY

A Century of Change

In 1809 Richard Sheridan watched his playhouse, the Theatre Royal at Drury Lane, burn to the ground in spite of the provision of an iron safety curtain that proved to be ineffectual when required. Wadding from muskets fired during a performance of *Pizarro* (1799) had set fire to the scenery depicting the Valley of the Torrent. The new century had witnessed few serious plays at this great theatre, for melodramas and spectacles entailing performing dogs, elephants and other creatures had replaced them. When phoenix-like the new theatre by Benjamin Dean Wyatt rose on the site in 1812 it was a four-tier house with a seating capacity of 2,283, a proscenium opening of 42 feet and a stage depth of 80 feet. On the size of both Drury Lane and Covent Garden the playwright Joanna Baillie remarked that 'the largeness of our two regular theatres, so unfavourable for hearing clearly, has changed in a great measure the character of pieces exhibited within their walls'.[1] The growing size of theatres, bringing in larger box office receipts, was replicated in other playhouses and the extension of melodrama and spectacle was to be seen not only in the legitimate buildings but also in the minor playhouses erected in the suburbs of the metropolis.

One must remember that the first half of the nineteenth century was an age of communication: two examples will show how this affected the theatres. First, in 1825 the Stockton and Darlington railway began to carry passengers and soon actor managers were taking their companies from one town to another, repeating a limited repertoire at a large number of touring houses. Second, by the beginning of the century both in London and the provinces newspapers carrying reports of theatre were to be had and as these grew in size and as journals with theatre columns detailing productions were established, so reports of plays tended to be less descriptive and critical writing became an art. Towards the end of the century the essays of Clement Scott were eagerly read in the *Telegraph*, although we might find them patronising today.

Running parallel with the vogue for theatrical criticism was the building or rebuilding of many small, minor theatres in London. In the past these had often housed melodramas – described loosely as 'blood and thunder plays' – and as long as the piece contained at least one song it was exempt from the limiting regulations affecting the legitimate drama. In 1843 the Theatres Act was passed and legitimate drama could be presented at houses other than those with a royal patent, as long as the text gained the approval of the Lord Chamberlain's Office. During the 1860s Tom Robertson was writing a new kind of domestic drama (facetiously called the 'cup and saucer theatre') within which 'fireside concerns' were aired. Whereas the earlier melodramas could be splattered with blood, in the Robertson era – one in which Arthur Wing Pinero and Henry Arthur Jones were also writing – gentility prevailed and families as a unit visited the theatre, a custom which altered the layout of the auditorium with the introduction of comfortable stalls at the front of the ground floor seating, made more luxurious by carpeting, and the provision of the 'family circle', one tier above the dress circle and less expensive.

The last couple of decades of the century saw an unexpected development: Henrik Ibsen and Anton Chekhov gave in translation to the British theatre plays which demanded careful thought and discussion, a trait which coincided with the provision in evening classes of lectures and readings on a range of arts subjects.

Melodrama

In 1802 the Covent Garden curtain rose on Thomas Holcroft's entertainment, *A Tale of Mystery*. It was a story of the activity of brigands: an attack on a morally good man left him without the power of speech and a chase ensued across wild, mountainous country. The resources of the scenic department at this theatre guaranteed a spectacular production and the large orchestra was put to good use as described in the *Monthly Mirror:*

> The composer [Thomas Busby] tells the story as well as the author. The characters are introduced with appropriate melodies; the progress of the scene is illustrated in a similar way; and every incident and feeling is marked by correspondent musical expression. In addition to this the subject of *The Tale of Mystery* demands the aid of pantomime [ie mime] and there is also an opportunity for spectacle and dance, so that beside the charm of novelty, this entertainment exhibits a combination of every thing that is calculated to please the eye and the ear, and, we may add with strict justice, to gratify the taste, and powerfully to interest the feelings of the public.[2]

If the music was carefully conceived, so were the scenes for various melodramas: the great name to conjure with was that of the Grieve family who for three generations delighted audiences with its elaborate scenery at the patent houses. There was a strong sense of geographic reality in the subjects such as snow mountains in Siberia by Thomas, the river Volga by moonlight (William) and by the paterfamilias, John Henderson – he worked for John Philip Kemble – the square in Moscow complete with its triumphal arch. Another designer, Clarkson Stanfield, not only devised layered scenery – the audience looked through cut areas of one layer after another on the peep scope principle – but also used the diorama on which scenes were painted and spied through an arch or similar conventional frame as one location changed to another. One of his great successes was a set of Venetian scenes based on sketches made whilst in the city, showing such well-known buildings as San Marco, the Bridge of Sighs and the Dogana for the pantomime *Harlequin and Little Thumb* (1831); later the diorama was cut up and utilised in *The Merchant of Venice* (*c.* 1596) and *Venice Preserv'd* (1682). Whilst the Grieves' and Stanfield's painters worked, the patent houses were in the process of changing from oil lamps to gas light which, once the artistic possibilities were mastered – at first the gas was turned on full blast drowning the high-pitched voice of the heroine – was highly artistic and subtle.

Romantic poets and playwriting

Partly as a reaction against melodrama some of the romantic poets wrote plays but although a few of these were accepted by the patent managements, their impact was slight compared with, say, Matthew Lewis. As might be expected, the protracted poetic diction of Samuel Taylor Coleridge slowed the action of his play *Remorse* (1813), in which Ordonio is confronted – the method of achieving this puzzled Coleridge greatly – by the supposedly murdered Alvar. From the start of the conjuration scene in which Alvar was to appear to his aggressor soft music was played on an '*instrument of glass or steel*' and mysterious voices sang in the area where a framed illumination would enact the crime, surrounded by the usual appurtenances such as cloudy incense and rising flames. Much of this had already been seen in Schiller's play *The Ghost Seer* and Coleridge may have had it in mind but in his own play the supernatural was transmuted to the region of magic and would have been improved if reserved for a pantomime.

Bertram by Charles Robert Maturin was staged by Edmund Kean at Drury Lane in 1816 with great success, although disliked by the Tory newspapers as the remark in the *British Review* conveys:

> Rotten principles and a bastard sort of sentiment, such in short, as have been imported into this country from German moralists and poets, form the interest of this stormy and extravagant composition.[3]

With a nod to *Twelfth Night* and *The Tempest* the play began with thunder, lightning, rain and wind heard from within a seaside monastery; suddenly the scene opened out, showing by the light of flares monks clambering over the rocks searching for the victims of a shipwreck, moments which were 'sublimely grand and picturesque' in the balanced praise of the *Theatrical Inquisitor*.[4]

1819 saw the publication of *The Cenci* by Percy Bysshe Shelley, a tale of parricide and incestuous rape at which again the charge of volubility has to be made, to which might be added there is also an unacknowledged debt to Shakespeare, especially in the speech of Beatrice:

> So young to go
> Under the obscure, cold, rotting, wormy ground!
>   (Act 5, scene 4)

bringing to mind Claudio's speech in *Measure for Measure* (Act 3, scene 1). Echoes of *Macbeth* are also heard. The themes of incest and atheism seemed to attract Shelley as he concentrates on the innate evil of Count Francesco Cenci. The play was first mounted by the Shelley Society in 1886 and later, in 1959, enjoyed performances at the Old Vic with Barbara Jefford as Beatrice.

Bad men featured too in William Wordsworth's attempt at playwriting in *The Borderers*, which he aspired to produce at Covent Garden. Yet again the piece works as poetry but fails as theatre. Lord Byron is represented by *Werner*, first produced by Charles William Macready at Drury Lane in 1830 after cutting more than half the lines. The romantic poets were not really the stuff of which playwrights are made but in their own right as poets they figure later in the survey.

The stage setting

By 1830 the long reign of melodrama was coming to an end and many of the principles for which it had stood were seen as dated and simplistic. The gap between landowner and cottager had been stressed in rural settings, and in urban locations management were many cuts above their employees. Virtue had lain in the hearts of the poor and the dispossessed prompting sentimentality in the drama. Theatrical predestination had demanded that the villain should be permanently tarnished, whilst at the other end of the mantelpiece hero and heroine had pursued a sober and godly life. The ascendancy of the common populace would take over from the melodrama but this did not happen until the 1860s. How was the gap filled?

Strangely, with the exploration of the lower strata of society the stage picture and the mechanics of creating it came to the fore. From 1831 to 1839 Eliza Vestris, a dancer, managed the Olympic Theatre in Wych Street, off the Strand. In this small building she determined to create the illusion of reality on the stage. The old system of shutters, wings and borders had been criticised and Vestris decided that box sets should be used. For an interior these consisted of three walls of a room complete with functional doors and windows topped by a ceiling with the proscenium arch acting as a frame for the 'picture': the experiment was put to work in 1832 and perfected by the end of the decade for a production of Dion Boucicault's *The London Assurance* (1841). Victorian prompt books refer to the setting as a 'chamber with raking flats'. Vestris's second husband, Charles Mathews, junior, wrote of his wife's attention to detail:

> Drawing-rooms were fitted up like drawing rooms, and furnished with care and taste. Two chairs no longer indicated that two persons were to be seated...[5]

It took a little longer to solve the problems of portraying the airiness of the outdoor setting but by 1863 an article in *All the Year Round*, a magazine edited by Charles Dickens, described the possibilities:

> [Here] the sky will close the scene in overhead: an unbroken canopy extending from a certain point behind the proscenium and high above it, over the stage, and away to where, at the extreme backward limit of the theatre, it mingles softly with the horizon...this great arched canopy, spanning the stage from side to side, and from front to back, will lend itself to all sorts of beautiful and truthful effects.

But what plays were used to demonstrate the new interest in realism? Vestris employed James Robinson Planché to write comedies for the Olympic performed by a handpicked coterie of comedians, including her husband. The insistence on realism combined with exquisite taste opened the way for Squire and Marie Bancroft to present elegant revivals and new plays when they made the Prince of Wales' their home in the 1860s.

Shakespeare with scenery

The appreciation of spectacular settings was allied to an enthusiasm for Shakespeare's plays and – strange bedfellows – the two developed together in part due to the enthusiasm of Queen Victoria. She had a fondness for the acting of Charles Kean, son of Edmund, whose *Richard III* in the Colley Cibber version she went to see:

> The manner in which he gave 'So much for Buckingham' was truly splendid, and called down thunders of applause, as also many other of the scenes where he gets very much excited; he fought and died beautifully. He was uncommonly well disguised, and looked very deformed and wicked.[6]

Later, at Christmas 1848, Victoria decided to have a temporary theatre built in the Rubens Room at Windsor Castle and called on Kean to select actors from several different companies to form a cast for each presentation. The first choice was *The Merchant of Venice* (*c*. 1596) in which the tragedian played Shylock and the productions continued until the death of Prince Albert in 1861. Victoria's royal patronage was not a personal indulgence but a decision on the part of the monarch to show the importance of English drama, at the time in danger of becoming submerged by visiting foreign opera and dramatic companies.[7]

When Kean was neither at Windsor nor touring, his London base was the Princess' Theatre in Oxford Street. There, between 1850 and 1859, he mounted spectacular Shakespeare. Coal gas was used to light these productions to brilliant effect. The management years coincided with the Great Exhibition of 1851 when science was used as an aid in artistic presentation: this, as mentioned, was the time of the panorama and the diorama which in the hands of the Grieves would give the impression that the stage with its newly found flexibility was moving towards cinema-photography. Thus in *A Midsummer Night's Dream* (*c.* 1595) Kean introduced a moving panorama behind the lovers as they tramped through the wood outside Athens. But when the supernatural world impinged on the stage the critic J W Cole saw there a romanticism which today cloys:

> ...the first appearance of Oberon and Titania, with their attendant trains; the noiseless footsteps of the dance on the moonlit greensward, with the shadowed reflection of every rapid and graceful movement; the wood peopled with its innumerable fairy legions, whose voices lull their queen to sleep upon a bank of flowers...[8]

Not all was sweetness and light in Kean's productions. A painting by Alfred Elmore depicts Macbeth's banqueting hall at the point of the appearance of Banquo's ghost. Although the stage is full of incident – bards with harps in the gallery for instance – one sees unity and focus. The ghost appears centrally by rising from behind the table and exits in the same manner and at the end of the episode the setting 'dissolves into a mist'. But there were incidents which did not ring true and Frederick Robson put on a burlesque of the production with words by the playwright Judge Thomas Talfourd and a selection of black minstrel tunes, which for the porter's scene, included, 'Who's dat knocking on de door?' There could be in Kean's work strange interpolations, such as the corps of fairies dancing on the return of Henry V after the Battle of Agincourt. However, it is worth remembering that Kean was more than a knockabout showman: his father had sent him to Eton and later he became a Fellow of the Society of Antiquaries.

At much the same time as Kean was working in Oxford Street Samuel Phelps was presenting Shakespeare at Sadler's Wells Theatre in Clerkenwell. His work was less elaborate than that of Kean and in the presentations he was aided by the actor turned artist, Frederick Fenton. Here also the stage was lit by gas and one of Fenton's innovations appeared in *A Midsummer Night's Dream* (*c*. 1595), a seamless blue net the size of the act drop, used as a transparency. He employed a double diorama for this play, the first layer representing a cut-wood showing foliage and tree trunks and the second presented slowly drifting clouds. Phelps' range of Shakespeare plays at Sadler's Wells included a number of rarely performed works such as *Timon of Athens* (*c*. 1607) and *Pericles* (*c*. 1606).

It was the proud boast of both Kean and Phelps that the costumes were as authentic as the scenes and accordingly designers of quality were employed. J R Planché, for example, designed those for Kean's *King John*, although there was a degree of approximation. Women's costumes, by the dictates of modesty, tended to be much bulkier in the skirts than they should have been.

'Naturalism': poverty and depravity

A variety of sources provided plots for plays between the years 1840 and 1880. Within the area of fiction as Charles Dickens' novels appeared in serial form the narrative was shaped into one or more plays. Factually, gleanings from the newspapers about criminal activities such as the exploits of Sweeney Todd and the death of Maria Marten were profitable source materials.

Tom Taylor, for some time the editor of *Punch*, drew on the themes of the urban poor, the criminal classes and domestic lives for *Still Waters Run Deep* (1855) – in which the audience learnt that illicit love was a fact of life – and *The Ticket of Leave Man* (1863). The latter play made a name for itself by beginning with a crowded restaurant within which the audience was immediately introduced to the underworld. Taylor was also interested in history and combined this with the theatre in some episodes from the life of Peg Woffington, a seventeenth-century actress, under the title *Masks and Faces* (1852).

Dion Boucicault dealt with the extremes of the town's fashionables, as in *The London Assurance*, and the urban poor in his variants on *The Streets of London* (1857), which became *The Poor of Liverpool* (1864) and *The Poor of the London Streets* (1866). However, it was in his Irish settings that his plays were the most lasting, such as *The Colleen Bawn* (1860), *Arrah-na-Pogue* (1864) and *The Shaughran* (1874), all three sentimental and melodramatic but reflecting the lives of people far enough from London to be lilting and interesting.

As we advance through naturalism we meet the plays of Tom Robertson, an actor before he became a dramatist. His aim was to reproduce the language one heard outside the theatre in drawing rooms and public places. By now it has become dated but when Robertson's plays first appeared there was a vitality and freshness in the dialogue, to the extent that surprise was expressed that an audience heard in the theatre 'what they hear in their own houses'.[9] Allied to the words are unusually full stage directions. George D'Alroy has inflicted a shock on his mother in *Caste* (1867) and Robertson gives a detailed sketch of the reactions of the Marchioness and those around her:

> *George*: My wife!
> *Marchioness*: Married!
> *George*: Married.
> [*The Marchioness sinks into an easychair. George replaces Esther on sofa, but still retains her hand. Three hesitating taps at door are heard. George crosses to door, opens it, discovers Eccles, who enters. George drops down back of Marchioness's chair.*]

Several effects are obtained from these directions. Movements and gestures are used to reinforce the meaning of the spoken word. But there is more than this: the playwright has maintained a control of the total stage picture: here again we are looking to the film-making of the future. Robertson's plays are sentimental in the way that melodramas often were half a century earlier but there is a serious intention underlying them and a genuine striving for total integration. The theme of the play, as opposed to the plot, may be seen in the single word titles Robertson gave to each: *Society* (1865), *Ours* (1866), *Play* (1868) and *School* (1869).

The productions were certainly polished, one of the advantages of their staging at the Prince of Wales' Theatre in Tottenham Street then under the management of the Bancrofts. They offered Robertson the opportunity to direct his own writing, in his experienced hands an added advantage. The husband and wife team had adopted a policy of presenting a single play for a run rather than continuing the repertory system, allowing considerably more time for rehearsal and the subsequent possibility of attention to detail. It became customary, too, for London managements to take productions on tour to the provinces, often on a repertory basis. However, Robertson took one play at a time with the above advantages. Although there was a general approval of *Caste*, one finds dissensions, especially amongst playwrights. After seeing it W B Yeats berated the roles:

Two of the minor persons had a certain amount of superficial characterisation, as if out of the halfpenny comic papers; but the central persons, the men and the women that created the dramatic excitement, such as it was, had not characters of any kind, being vague ideals, perfection as it is imagined by a commonplace mind. The audience could give them its sympathy without the labour that comes from awakening knowledge.

The last sentence is a point to bear in mind when reading the play.

Sir Arthur Wing Pinero and Henry Arthur Jones

It happened that a few weeks later
Her aunt was off to the Theatre
To see that Interesting Play
The Second Mrs Tanqueray (1893)[10]

Whatever Matilda's aunt made of Pinero's play, it was the apex of a series of farces by means of which Arthur Pinero learnt the craft of dramatic construction. However banal a scenario of the plot seems, the drama effectively functioned on the stage as a story of deception and discovery that ended in tragedy with the suicide of Paula Tanqueray, successfully played by Mrs Patrick Campbell. It is worth remembering that the characters in *The Magistrate* (1885) – a far cry from the spirit of *Tanqueray* – pass through the same kind of hoops, although disguise is added to deception; but in both the preservation of respectability is highly important. After the first night the critic of *The Theatre* conferred on Pinero the accolade of the 'greatest of living dramatists' with which he combined the creation of a 'piece of literature'.[11] Some sentimental dramas each served as a maquette for Pinero's essay in biography and theatre history, a study of the ideas and aspirations of Tom Robertson under the title *Trelawney of the Wells* (1898). A strange mix of pathos and broad comedy had been blended but the audience gained the impression that although its members were looking back thirty years, it was as if the retrospection was projected to the present. As in Robertson's plays, dialogue and construction had been thoroughly mastered.

Whether Henry Arthur Jones should be included in this survey is a moot point. In earlier days he was often compared with Pinero, with the conclusion 'Pinero for construction and Jones for dialogue'. Of Welsh descent, Jones was the son of a Buckinghamshire farmer, a member of a dissenting family and by early trade a shop assistant, elements which may be discovered in his plays. His first work, *The Silver King* (1882), neglected for many years, has lately been given productions by amateur companies but its popularity in its day may be judged by the £18,000 in royalties Jones earned from the text. Although melodramatic, the play treats seriously problems of relationships and more often those of man to God, rather than at the level of man to man as often explored in the 1880s. Infrequently staged, one of his strongest theatrical pieces is *Mrs Dane's Defence* (1900), in which the dialogue is nervous and the interrogation of Mrs Dane by Sir Daniel Carteret in the third act strong and carefully mounting in tension as he digs to discover the truth about the identity of the woman.

Foreign influences on British drama

The insularity of Britain did not isolate it from the ideals of a couple of foreign playwrights. First there was Henrik Ibsen. Part of the corpus of his work is concerned with the furtherance of naturalism and a representative play is *A Doll's House* (1879), a study of the relationship between a lawyer, Torvald Helmer, and his wife Nora, whom Helmer views merely as a plaything, a doll. The effect, wrote August Strindberg, was to reveal that marriage was 'a far from divine institution, people stopped regarding it as an automatic provider of absolute bliss, and divorce between incompatible parties came at last to be accepted as conceivably justified'.[12] The successor to *A Doll's House* was *Ghosts* (1881), a study of the breakdown of family life under the impact of venereal disease. *An Enemy of the People* (1882) represents naturalism on a wider scale, the effect of a polluted water supply on a small town, expressed through the rivalry existing between two brothers in their public *personae* as Mayor and Officer of Health. These ideas on the presentation of a public self and the exploration of the 'reality' lying beneath this helped to shape the ideas and content of Shaw, Barker and Galsworthy to name only a trio of future writers of the twentieth century. But naturalism was not the only factor in Ibsen's work; this is balanced by symbolism in other plays. At times the symbolism becomes the *raison d'être* for the play: take *The Master Builder* (1892) for example; here the buildings of Solness mean more than a series of constructions but represent the whole commitment of his life and his fulfilment. Later Freud and Jung were to assert that the liberation of a person can only come from within which seems to be true of Solness, just as the final slamming of the door (the sound with which each of Ibsen's plays ends is a symbol in itself) in *A Doll's House* represents Nora's emancipation.

In the plays of Anton Chekhov one finds a highly subtle blend of naturalism suffused with lyricism and symbol and this trio of characteristics influenced British drama reinforcing the impact of Ibsen. In Chekhov's plays a narrative line is barely discernable; instead we are aware of the passage of time and of a strange *ennui* that envelops the people who are virtually waiting. As evening falls in *Uncle Vanya* (1899) Sonia places candles on the table and tells Vanya:

> We shall go on living, Uncle Vanya. We shall live through a long, long succession of days and tedious evenings. We shall patiently suffer the trials which fate imposes on us; we shall work for others, now and in our old age, and we shall have no rest.[13]

There is a lyrical poignancy in this view of living and yet in the theatre it works its pathos on the audience; its members are simply gazing at 'scenes from country life'.

The Seagull (1896) and *The Cherry Orchard* (1904) are written on a larger scale. Each is set on an estate in need of renovation. At the beginning of the former an outdoor stage is in the process of construction, a symbol of the lure of the theatre which attracts Nina just as a generation earlier it drew Irena Arkadina. The title itself is symbolic referring also to Nina with a strong hint of tragedy in the parallel of the seagull which Trepliov kills. It is around such an atmosphere and these sort of icons that Chekhov builds his work rather than allowing a series of actions to take over the primacy of the piece. Yet strangely the playwright refers to each of these two plays as a comedy, a description which has puzzled many directors, especially as in each such message as it gives is reinforced in the last moments by a sound redolent of violence: there is the shot which destroys Trepliov in *The Seagull* and the sound of the destruction of the orchard in the second piece. Chekhov takes the audience beyond the categorisation of his work and beyond a narrative line; often the play seems to be internal to the characters.

Konstantin Stanislavsky was one of the most successful of the directors of Chekhov's work, especially in his productions with the Moscow Arts Theatre. In addition to the rehearsals he built up a series of studio exercises in which the company took part, where some emotional situations were worked 'for real'.

Poetry

The plays of the nineteenth century, whether they were acted or not, have been given priority of space and so we deal but briefly with poetry and the novel but that does not infer that these two genres are of lesser importance; in fact, the nineteenth century was the great age for the composition of Romantic poetry. William Wordsworth, by then an established poet, made his home in the Lake District in 1798 to be joined within a couple of years by Samuel Taylor Coleridge and Robert Southey. Before the move Wordsworth and Coleridge had already collaborated on the first edition of *Lyrical Ballads* (1798). 'The Rime of the Ancient Mariner' was Coleridge's principal contribution to the book and to Wordsworth's lot fell 'Lines written a few miles above Tintern Abbey', a heralding of the Industrial Revolution. In the Preface Wordsworth explained that the published poems were an attempt to fit 'to metrical arrangement a selection of the real language of men in a state of vivid sensation'. Two further poems of Coleridge, both capturing the imagination of the period, were 'Kubla Khan' and 'Christabel'.

Sir Walter Scott's output of prose romances was preceded by his ballads which he wrote with the passion of an antiquarian: *Marmion* (1808), *The Lady of the Lake* (1810) and *Rokeby* (1813) are examples. They were hurried works but redolent of mediaeval atmosphere.

Lord George Byron also dashed off works with speed. *Beppo* (1818), written in *ottava rima*, was a Venetian story in rhyme and *Manfred* (1817) had a brief success on the London stage. A lashing tongue was a lasting aid to satiric writing: in *The Vision of Judgement* (1822) Robert Southey, the Poet Laureate, was pilloried and Farmer George, a popular appellation in Berkshire for George III who regularly gathered mushrooms at daybreak in Windsor Great Park. Byron sold the ruinous Newstead Abbey in Nottinghamshire, part of his inheritance, spending much of the money to further his Italian travels. His wide output of poetry and drama was influential in Europe.

Perhaps it was his tuberculosis that heightened experience and the visual world for John Keats. 'The Eve of St Agnes', a sumptuous mediaeval story, catches colours like facets of glass:

A casement high and triple-arch'd there was,
All garlanded with carven imag'ries
Of fruits, and flowers, and bunches of knot grass,
And diamonded with panes of quaint device,
Innumerable of stains and splendid dyes,
As are the tiger-moth's deep-damask'd wings...

Here is the verse form of Edmund Spenser, himself a master of word painting. Next to this lengthy poem there are the odes, 'To Autumn', 'To a Nightingale' and 'On a Grecian Urn' which again present cool pictures combined with philosophy. The latter poem reminds us that the Marbles, the frieze from the Temple of Pallas Athene on the Acropolis, were brought to London in this century by Lord Elgin and deposited in the British Museum.

Poet Laureate for 42 years, Alfred Tennyson, after an initial disappointment, became the much-lauded rocklike stability England needed throughout the various crises of faith and politics in his lifetime. His name became a household word with the publication of *The Idylls of the King* (1859), a telling in blank verse of the Arthurian legend. The untimely death of his friend Arthur Hallam prompted the writing of *In Memoriam* (1850), a spiritual autobiography. By no means his finest work, 'The Charge of the Light Brigade' (1854) with its jingoistic sentiments again boasted a popular appeal. His short, simple pieces show the strength of his work in the use of monosyllabic words as in, 'Break, break, break.' One must remember too that his eye and ear were perfectly attuned to nature which, again using a simplicity of diction, is presented with clarity and genuineness:

...beneath a whispering rain
Night slid down one long stream of sighing wind.

Slow in coming to the fore, during the 1850s Robert Browning was known as 'Mrs Browning's husband', a reference to his poet-wife Elizabeth Barrett Browning. In his youth the family had lived in Camberwell, near to Dulwich Picture Gallery, with its collection of Italian Renaissance paintings, a strong influence on the mind-set of the future poet. Whether or not they were admitted as such, the strength of his writing lay in his dramatic lyrics, especially such character pieces as 'My last Duchess' (1842), 'Fra Lippo Lippi' (1855), 'The Bishop orders his tomb at St Praxed's Church' (1845), all ripe for solo performance. Whilst he was living in Florence, Browning discovered a transcript of an eighteenth-century murder trial that he used as the source for a set of twelve dramatic monologues, *The Ring and the Book* (1868–9). By the time of his death Browning enjoyed the same kind of stature as Tennyson: he had experimented with language and syntax and developed the dramatic monologue as an art form.

Unread and unpublished in his lifetime, Gerard Manley Hopkins, in spite of his obtuseness of expression, enjoys an eager following nowadays. A convert from Anglicanism, he became a Jesuit priest and renounced the writing of poetry, luckily a resolution he did not keep. The natural world, country people, baroque religious culture and at times sheer pessimism all provided grist for his poetry mill. Hopkins evolved a form of writing known as 'sprung rhythm' which presents the speaker of his work with a challenge. Letters to the Rev Richard Dixon explain the principles on which this works and are often quoted in the preface to anthologies of Hopkins's work.

Oscar Wilde serves as a representative of the 'art for art's sake' movement. After serving his prison sentence at Reading Wilde found refuge in France where he wrote *The Ballad of Reading Gaol* (1898), a fine poem about the killing of an unfaithful lass, in which is the summary line 'Yet each man kills the thing he loves.' Like-minded writers of this literary coterie were much influenced by the French Symbolists, Baudelaire, Verlaine and Mallarmé.

The novel

If the plays are essays in naturalism, can we expect the novels to have a similar aim? Not quite. One reason for this is the guidance, some would say intrusion, of the authorial voice. Who is manipulating the characters? Who comments on the shaping of the plot?

Jane Austen's novels consist of domestic life written on a small scale. Not for her the background of the wars with France and America or the social traumas of the Industrial Revolution; instead we are given pictures of country estates broadening out into life in Bath, a city and society she disliked. *Pride and Prejudice* (1813) is the novel in which the characters are the most firmly and colourfully drawn, offering strong narrative lines about the tensions and suspense involved in the art of seeking a matrimonial partner. Moving away from her usual *métier* Austen interested herself in a gentle parody of the gothic novel in *Northanger Abbey* (1818) and it is fascinating to compare this with the work of an accomplished gothic enthusiast such as Mrs Ann Radcliffe in *The Mysteries of Udolpho* (1794) or for that matter with the more caustic satire of Thomas Love Peacock's *Nightmare Abbey* (1818).

Mary Shelley's was the sole excursion into the horrors of early nineteenth-century science fiction in *Frankenstein* (1818), the story of an inventor, Dr Frankenstein, who creates a nameless monster that, as with the work of most over-reachers, gets out of hand. That section in which the monster escapes from his master and makes his way across the wide spaces of Russia and Tartary, drained of all colour, is the most atmospheric.

A significant picture of life in London is gained from Pierce Egan's book of the same name (1821) in which the trio of 'Corinthian Tom', Jerry Hawthorn, up from the country, and Bob Logic, an Oxonian, sample the delights of the capital, taking in such aspects of Regency life as a visit to a royal palace and boxing lessons from the famous pugilist 'Gentleman' Jackson. Hot on the novel's publication it was dramatised and received stage presentations. The names of two of the characters, Tom and Jerry, were commemorated in the name of a punch consisting of hot rum and eggs, as well as in a later series of cartoon film-shorts.

Under many guises the life and character of Charles Dickens has been scrutinised: we know that he had a burning enthusiasm for both the professional and amateur theatre as well as for the one-man-show which is what his histrionic readings were, in spite of the ostensible reliance on a script and desk. There were too the amateur theatricals – presented at such locations as the Gallery of Illustration, Regent Street, and Rockingham Castle – of a variety of plays including a couple especially written by his friend Wilkie Collins for his company of enthusiasts. Studies have also been written of the transference from page to stage of his novels, profuse in their publication.

Dickens' writings contain numbers of descriptions of theatrical life. In *Nicholas Nickleby* (1838–9) there is the interlude in which Nicholas meets Vincent Crummles and his 'thespian galaxy', an episode enhanced by the drawings of D'Hablot Brown (known as 'Phiz') showing the interior of the theatre at Portsmouth. In the illustrations one of the performers of Thomas Collins' company, Mr Floyer, appears in fictional habits as Mr Folair. *Hard Times* (1854) is set in the smoke blackened landscape of Coketown, splashed with the garish colour provided by Sleary's Circus:

> The clashing and banging band attached to the horse-riding establishment which had there set up its rest

in a wooden pavilion was in full bray. A flag, floating from the summit of the temple, proclaimed to mankind that it was 'Sleary's Horse-Riding' which claimed their suffrages. Sleary himself, a stout modern statue with a money-box at its elbow, in an ecclesiastical niche of early gothic architecture, took the money.[14]

Astley's Amphitheatre in Westminster Bridge Road, home of Woolford's troupe of horses, is given in word pictures in *Sketches by Boz* (1836–7), with rather more interest in the parties making up the audience than in the performers. It appears again when the Nubbles family have a night out at Astley's completed by supper at an oyster shop:

…[Astley's] with all the paint, gilding, and looking glass; the vague smell of horses suggestive of coming wonders; the curtain that hid such gorgeous mysteries; the clean white sawdust down in the circus; the company coming in and taking their places; the fiddlers looking carelessly up at them…What a glow was that, which burst upon them all, when that long, clear, brilliant row of lights came slowly up; and what the feverish excitement when the little bell rang and the music began in good earnest, with strong parts for the drums, and sweet effects for the triangles!

This is enough to demonstrate that Dickens was totally at home amongst the world of entertainment and amply able to play his own part within it.

The Brontë family, working in the parsonage at Haworth, tramped over home ground in their novels. Charlotte used her own experiences in *Jane Eyre* (1847), setting much of it within the gothic house of Thornfield where the master was the Byronic Mr Rochester; beneath the activity lies Charlotte's insistence on the equality of the sexes. In like vein Emily Brontë's *Wuthering Heights* (1847) features as the title role a further gothic manor house. A shocked reaction followed publication as critics found the book amoral, coarse and violent; nevertheless the writing was powerful and still draws a literary response.

Three novelists whose work was much admired in their day deserve a comment. George Eliot, the pseudonym of Mary Ann Evans, wrote *The Mill on the Floss* in 1860, a book which has received a number of dramatisations. Critics found that she had analysed 'the interior of the mind' of each of her principal characters and the expression of the intense relationship between Maggie Tulliver and her brother was a thread in the work to be admired. Lewis Carroll was a mathematics don at Christ Church, Oxford, whose penchant for telling stories to small girls gave him an immortality in the publication of one of these, *Alice's Adventures in Wonderland* (1865). The dream quality is sustained throughout the story and some of the characters resemble children's toys. The countryside around Oxford is transformed into childlike patterns, such as the fields of Otmoor presented as a chequer board. In contrast the Wessex landscape shaped the imagination of Thomas Hardy and it is in *Tess of the D'Urbervilles* (1891) that the reader is given the most magnificent scenarios and settings, especially in the arraignment of the heroine – and murderer – amongst the pillars of Stonehenge. As the novel comes to a close the Olympian gods peer down on the little-changed city of Winchester, reducing the participants of the drama to a set of puppets.

Near the start of this survey of the nineteenth century novel Mary Shelley's *Frankenstein* was mentioned. At the end of the century Bram Stoker – the stage manager for the great actor-manager Sir Henry Irving – wrote a gothic horror story *Dracula* (1897) set in London and Transylvania; there are references to Whitby in the book, too, a place in which Stoker did much of his planning whilst lodging on the West Cliff (the house is denoted by a blue plaque) although the writing was achieved at Cruden Bay in Scotland whilst staying at the Kilmarnock Inn. The plot presents the reader with a study in vampirism. The form of the narrative is interesting, harking back to the eighteenth-century novel with its frames of letters, journals, telegrams and diaries. Yet again, adaptations for the stage have been made of the novel – the Scottish playwright Liz Lochhead scripted one such in which the place of women in society and their relationship with one another, leading in the play to suggestions of lesbianism, was a feature – as well as film versions, with *Bram Stoker's Dracula* (1992) as a recent example.

2.   SELECTED AUTHORS, POETS AND PLAYWRIGHTS

Note: Titles of plays are preceded by an asterisk.

1798:   Lyrical Ballads by William Wordsworth and Samuel Taylor Coleridge

1800:   *Mary Stuart by Schiller

1802:   *A Tale of Mystery by Thomas Holcroft

    1805:   Battle of Trafalgar and the death of Admiral Lord Nelson

    Master Betty (a child tragedian) mania

1805:   The Lay of the Last Minstrel by Walter Scott

1807:   Tales from Shakespeare by Charles and Mary Lamb

    1807:   Abolition of the slave trade

1808:   Marmion by Walter Scott

    1809:   Drury Lane accidentally burnt down

1811: The Regency begins

1812: Napoleon's march on Moscow

1812: War between Great Britain and the United
States of America

1813: Pride and Prejudice by Jane Austen

1813: *Remorse by Samuel Taylor Coleridge and
*The Miller and His Men by Isaac Pocock

1814: Waverley by Walter Scott

1815: Battle of Waterloo and the Congress of Vienna

1816: Kubla Khan by Samuel Taylor Coleridge

1818: Opening of Royal Coburg Theatre

1818: Northanger Abbey by Jane Austen;
Nightmare Abbey by Thomas Love Peacock;
Frankenstein by Mary Shelley

1820: George IV accedes

1820: The Eve of St Agnes by John Keats

1825: The Life of an Actor by Pierce Egan

1828: *Luke the Labourer by John Buckstone

1829: *Black Ey'd Susan by Douglas Jerrold

1830: William IV accedes

1832: Poems, Chiefly Lyrical by Alfred Tennyson

1836: Pickwick Papers by Charles Dickens

1837: Victoria accedes

1837: Oliver Twist by Charles Dickens begins in serial form

1838: Nicholas Nickleby by Charles Dickens begins in serial
form

1838: *The Lady of Lyons by Bulwer Lytton

1840: Marriage of Queen Victoria and Prince Albert

1841: *The London Assurance by Dion Boucicault

1841: The Old Curiosity Shop by Charles Dickens

1843: Theatre monopoly ended by Theatre
Regulation Act

1843:   A Christmas Carol by Charles Dickens

1847:   Jane Eyre by Charlotte Brontë;
        Wuthering Heights by Emily Brontë

     1848:   Royal theatricals begin at Windsor Castle

1850:   In Memoriam by Alfred Tennyson

     1851:   The Great Exhibition

1852:   *The Corsican Brothers by Thomas Taylor and
        Charles Reade

     1854:   Crimean War begins

1854:   Hard Times by Charles Dickens

1859:   A Tale of Two Cities by Charles Dickens

1860:   The Mill on the Floss by George Eliot

     1861:   United States Civil War begins

1863:   *The Ticket-of-Leave Man by Thomas Taylor

1864:   Dramatis Personae by Robert Browning

1864:   *David Garrick by Thomas Robertson

     1865:   United States Civil War ends and Abraham
        Lincoln assassinated

     1865:   Beginning of the Bancrofts' management of the
        Prince of Wales' Theatre

1865:   Alice in Wonderland by Lewis Carroll

1867:   *Caste by Thomas Robertson

1869:   Idylls of the King by Alfred Tennyson

1871:   *The Bells by Leopold Lewis in which Henry Irving
        appeared

1879:   *A Doll's House by Henrik Ibsen at the Danish
        Royal Theatre

1882:   *The Silver King by Henry Arthur Jones

1886:   The Mayor of Casterbridge by Thomas Hardy

1892:   * Lady Windermere's Fan by Oscar Wilde

1893:   *The Second Mrs Tanqueray by Arthur Wing Pinero

1895:   *An Ideal Husband by Oscar Wilde

1895:   *The Importance of being Earnest by Oscar Wilde

1897:   *Candida by George Bernard Shaw

1897:   Dracula by Bram (Abraham) Stoker

1898:   *Mrs Warren's Profession by George Bernard Shaw

1898:   The Ballad of Reading Gaol by Oscar Wilde

1901:   Death of Queen Victoria; acceded by Edward VII

3.   BIBLIOGRAPHY

General works

Archer, W, *The Old Drama and the New*. New York: Dodd, Mead and Co, 1926.

Boas, F S, *From Richardson to Pinero*. London: J Murray [1936].

Cook, Edward Dutton, *A Book of the Play*. London: Sampson Low, Marston, Searle and Rivington, 1881.

Disher, M Wilson, *Blood and Thunder: Mid-Victorian Melodrama and its Origins*. London: Muller [1949].

Herford, C H, *The Age of Wordsworth*. London: George Bell and Sons, 1922.

Lucas, F L, *Decline and Fall of the Romantic Ideal*. Cambridge: Cambridge University Press [1948].

Morley, Henry, *Journal of a London Playgoer*. Leicester: Leicester University Press, 1974.

Praz, Mario, *The Romantic Agony*. London: Oxford University Press, 2nd edition, 1970.

'The Provinces as a Dramatic School', in the *Saturday Review*, 66 (1888), 433–4.

Rosenfeld, Sybil, *A Short History of Scene Design in Great Britain*. Oxford: Basil Blackwell [1973].

Rowell, G, *The Victorian Theatre*. London: Oxford University Press, 1956.

Playwrights and other writers: biography, criticism and collected works

Jane Austen

Lascelles, Mary, *Jane Austen and her Art*. London: Oxford University Press, 1995.

Charlotte and Emily Brontë

Allott, M, ed, *The Brontës: The Critical Heritage*. London: Routledge and Kegan Paul, 1974.

Robert Browning

Hudson, G R, *Robert Browning's Literary Life*. Austin: Eakin, 1993.

George Gordon Lord Byron

Graham, P W, *Lord Byron*. 1998.

Lewis Carroll

Gardner, Martin, ed, *The Annotated Alice*. London: Penguin, 2001.

Samuel Taylor Coleridge

Fruman, N, *Coleridge: The Damaged Archangel*. London: Allen and Unwin, 1972.

Lowes, J Livingstone, *The Road to Zanadu*. New York: The Limited Editions Club, 1945.

Charles Dickens

Butt, John and Tillotson, Kate, *Dickens at Work*. London: Methuen, 1968.

Johnson, Edgar and Eleanor, *The Dickens Theatrical Reader*. London: Victor Gollancz Ltd, 1964.

Pierce Egan

Sales, R, 'Pierce Egan and the Representation of London' in P W Martin and R Jarvis, eds, *Reviewing Romanticism*. Basingstoke: Macmillan, 1992.

George Eliot (Mary Ann Evans)

Rignall, J ed, *The Oxford Reader's Companion to George Eliot*. Oxford: Oxford University Press, 2001.

Thomas Hardy

Sumner, R, *Thomas Hardy*. London: Macmillan, 1981.

Gerard Manley Hopkins

Hopkins, Gerard Manley, *Gerard Manley Hopkins*, ed W H Gardner. Harmondsworth: Penguin Books, 1953.

Martin, Robert Bernard, *Gerard Manley Hopkins: A Very Private Life*. London: Flamingo, 1992.

Henry Arthur Jones

Cordell, R A, *Henry Arthur Jones and the Modern Drama*. New York: R Long and R R Smith, inc., 1932.

John Keats

Robert Gittings, *John Keats*. Harmondsworth: Penguin Books, 1971.

Charles Robert Maturin

Idman, Niilo, *Charles Robert Maturin: His Life and Works*. London: Constable and Co, 1923.

Smiles, Samuel, *Memoir and Correspondence of the Late John Murray*. London: Routledge, 1997.

Thomas Robertson

Pemberton, T E, *The Life and Writings of T W Robertson*. London: Richard Bentley and Son, 1893.

Savin, M, *Thomas William Robertson*. Providence, RI: Brown University, 1950.

Sir Walter Scott

Sutherland, J, *The Life and Critical Biography of Sir Walter Scott*. Oxford: Blackwell, 1995.

Mary Shelley

Mellor, A K, *Mary Shelley, Her Life, Her Fictions, Her Monsters*. London: Routledge, 1988.

Bram Stoker

Carter, M L, ed, *Dracula: The Vampire and the Critics*. Ann Arbour, Mich: UMI Research Press, *c.* 1988.

Alfred Lord Tennyson

Hair, D S, *Tennyson's Language*. London and Toronto: University of Toronto Press, 1991.

Francis, Elizabeth A, *Tennyson: A Collection of Critical Essays*. Englewood Cliffs: Prentice Hall, *c.* 1980.

Oscar Wilde

Vivian Holland, *Oscar Wilde and His World*. London: Thames and Hudson, 1960.

William Wordsworth

Bate, J, *Romantic Ecology: Wordsworth and the Environmental Tradition*. London: Routledge (1991).

Biographies of actors and designers

Marie and Squire Bancroft

Bancroft, Marie and Squire, *The Bancrofts*. London: J Murray, 1909.

Henry Irving

Archer, W, *Henry Irving: Actor and Manager*. Hamilton: Adams and Co, 1883.

Charles Kean

'Cole, J W' [pseud for Calcraft, J W], *The Life and Theatrical Times of Charles Kean*. London: 1860.

Strange, Edward F, 'The Scenery of Charles Kean's Plays and the Great Scene Painters of his Day' in *The Magazine of Art* (1901–2), 454–9 and 514–8.

Strange, Edward F, 'The English Stage' in *The Quarterly Review*, 155 (1883), 354–88.

Samuel Phelps

Coleman, John, *Memoirs of Samuel Phelps*. London: Remington and Co, 1886.

J R Planché

Planché, J R, *Recollections and Reflections*. Tinsley, 1872.

Ellen Terry

Terry, Ellen, *The Story of My Life*. London: 1907.

The social background

Mayhew, Henry, *London Labour and the London Poor*, ed. Victor Neuberg. Harmondsworth: Penguin Books, 1985.

Petrie, Charles, *The Victorians*. London: Eyre and Spottiswoode, 1960.

4.   POINTS FOR DISCUSSION

- How were English playwrights of the nineteenth century influenced by the plays of Ibsen and Chekov?

- Did stage scenery help to reinforce theatrical 'naturalism'?

- Is 'historicity' desirable in Shakespearean production? Give some examples of nineteenth-century practice.

- Do you consider that plays and novels about the emancipation of women prepared audiences for the event?

- From your knowledge of nineteenth-century poetry would you agree with William Wordsworth that it could be written in the 'real language of men'?

- Consider the part landscape and location played in the Victorian novel.

5.   NOTES AND REFERENCES

1   Joanna Baillie, *A Series of Plays in which it is attempted to delineate the stronger passions of the mind*. London: 1821, introduction.

2   *Monthly Mirror*, December 1802.

3   *British Review*, 8 (1816), 70.

4   *Theatrical Inquisitor*, May 1816.

5   Charles Dickens, ed, *The Life of Charles James Matthews Chiefly Autobiographical*. London: Macmillan and Co, 1870, 2. 76.

6   Viscount Esher, ed, *The Girlhood of Queen Victoria*. London: 1912, 1. 272.

7   An account of Queen Victoria's partiality for drama is given in Michael R Booth, 'Queen Victoria and the Theatre' in the *University of Toronto Quarterly*, 36 (1966–7), 249–58.

8   J W Cole, *The Life and Theatrical Times of Charles Kean*. London: Richard Bentley, 1859, 2. 109.

9   Thomas Purnell, *Dramatists of the Present Day*. London: Chapman and Hall, 1871, p 93.

10 Hilaire Belloc, 'Matilda'.

11 July 1893, pp 3–8.

12 August Strindberg, Preface to *Getting Married*, 1884, cited in Henrik Ibsen, *A Doll's House*, translated and with an Introduction by Michael Meyer. London: Eyre Methuen, 1965, p 15.

13 Act 4.

14 Book 1, chapter 3.

BRITAIN AND TWENTIETH-CENTURY EUROPE

1.   SURVEY

Theatre trends during the twentieth century

Writing at the beginning of the 1960s Professor Allardyce Nicoll hazarded a guess that one of the principal characteristics of offerings on the twentieth-century stage would appear to be eclecticism. Now that the century has run its course a pattern may be observed more clearly and to trace this with great brevity may help to place in context the various playwrights who feature. The selection of these given in this section is a personal one but I have been prompted to ask about each, 'Is this person's work still relevant, or of sufficient quality, to be performed with a degree of regularity?'

Towards the end of the nineteenth century Tom Robertson's plays helped to establish the vogue for realistic social dramas and this trend was continued into the twentieth century. John Galsworthy in his epic novels, especially *The Forsyte Saga* (1922), opened the front door onto a well-heeled family, a point brought out in the first television presentation (1967) of a dramatisation of a novel that was both leisurely and detailed. His plays, too, gave a view of a similar social strata. One notices an affinity with the plays of Harley Granville-Barker especially in *The Voysey Inheritance* (1905) and *The Madras House* (1910), both of which have been presented at the Royal National Theatre. Alongside these there are the plays of George Bernard Shaw continuing from the previous century, where in his trio of 'Plays Unpleasant' realism is thrust at the spectators: *Mrs Warren's Profession* (1902) brought them up against prostitution and *Widowers' Houses* (1892) highlighted the evils of slum dwellings. Admirable although these are, they taught audiences that too easily, the stage could be used as a platform for polemic and social propaganda.

In 1899 the Irish Literary Theatre was set into being through the inspiration of W B Yeats, J M Synge and Lady Augusta Gregory; four years later Dublin's Abbey Theatre opened. In their own way the writers providing material for this stage (Yeats, Synge, Sean O'Casey, Shaw and Padraic Colum) were assuredly aware of the tragedy that lay within the Irish rural landscape and plays on this theme followed; *Riders to the Sea* (John Millington Synge, 1905) a tale of an old woman and her drowned sons, has the power to move audiences today. To realism a poetic sadness had been added.

Under the enthusiastic guidance of Miss A E F Horniman, from the family of Horniman's Tea fame, the repertory movement was established at the end of the first decade of the century, with the earliest of the theatres founded in Dublin, Manchester, Glasgow, Liverpool and Birmingham. The usual pattern was for a theatre to stage a different play each week although as time went by this was presented for a longer period and eventually toured on a circuit system. Audiences declined after the second world war as television established itself in the home and cinemas grew more splendid and comfortable: a prime example of one of these is the Granada Theatre at Tooting in South London designed by Theodore Komisajevsky. Plays staged tended to be either written for repertory or reasonably successful west end plays that had terminated their opening run. A few repertory theatres remain; well-known examples are The Rep at Birmingham, the Citizens at Glasgow and the Stephen Joseph Theatre at Scarborough.

Comedy was not submerged by realism. Soon the comedy of manners, one of the characteristics of the Restoration, was reborn in the writing of Somerset Maugham (*The Circle*, 1921), Freddie Lonsdale (*The Last of Mrs Cheney*, 1925) and Sir Alan Herbert (*La Vie Parisienne*, 1929). The last time the clipped, pointed speaking had been heard on the London stage was in the comedies of Oscar Wilde.

Another interest of writers, the time-space theme which captured interest shortly before 1930, is best exemplified in the work of J B Priestley. The sense of return to an agreed point is strongly brought out in his plays such as *Time and the Conways* (1937), in turn reinforced by moral judgements in *An Inspector Calls* (1945), a play running in the West End as this book is being written.

Costume drama in the guise of historical plays, too, provided a colourful theatrical evening. Notable amongst these writers is John Drinkwater (*Abraham Lincoln*, 1918), Clifford Bax (*The Rose without a Thorn*, 1931) and Gordon Daviot (*Richard of Bordeaux*, 1932). The growing fondness during the 1930s for colour combined with historical accuracy prompted three female stage designers to band together under the name of Motley in order to design and produce both costumes and occasional settings.

Various attempts had been made at poetic drama but these were not lasting. However, in 1935 the United States responded with enthusiasm to *Winterset* by Maxwell Anderson, based on the trial of Nicola Sacco and Bartolomeo Vanzetti, two Italian anarchists, who in 1927 were convicted of murder in the United States after five years of litigation. In Britain T S Eliot's *Murder in the Cathedral* (1935) received its first production in the chapter house of Canterbury, a play based on the martyrdom of Thomas à Becket. Certain directorial problems were created by Eliot's use of a chorus comprised of the women of Canterbury, a convention which was later abandoned by both Eliot and his fellow playwrights, or the composite role was subsumed within a 'common man' of some sort as in Robert Bolt's play *A Man for all Seasons* (1960). Soon the Mercury Theatre in Notting Hill Gate was regularly staging experiments in the genre and during the second world war poetic drama was to receive a wider audience through radio, especially in the religious works of Dorothy L Sayers. Further plays of Eliot's such as *The Family Reunion* (1939), a play based on *The Eumenides* of Aeschylus and *The Cocktail Party* (1949) received west end presentations, although the poetic element in them was discreet. It was left to Christopher Fry to shower the audience with cataracts of alliteration and assonance in his highly successful commercial works, *The Lady's Not for Burning* (1948) and *Venus Observed* (1950). Come the Festival of Britain in 1951, Fry was commissioned to write the festival play, *A Sleep of Prisoners* (1951), a then contemporary version of the Civil War incarceration of soldiers in Burford Church in Oxfordshire: Fry's work was staged in a small dark church, St Thomas's, off Regent Street, which no longer stands.

Musical comedy (after the second world war known as 'the musical') is difficult to fit into a survey of this nature and many histories of drama, suspecting that frivolity replaces worthiness, omit the subject: a pity as it has, at very least, influenced the history of staging. Most musicals originated in New York and quickly made their way to London, although those of Noël Coward (*Bitter Sweet*, 1930) and Ivor Novello (*Careless Rapture*, 1936 and *The Dancing Years*, 1939) were indigenous. From the late

1940s inflations of plays with music added to the original script became popular: *My Fair Lady* (1956) by Lerner and Loewe with original help from Shaw is a successful example that also owes much to Cecil Beaton's designs. But numbers of small scale productions helped to establish the truly English musical; there was Sandy Wilson's *The Boy Friend* (1953), a parody of musicals popular in the 1920s, and *Salad Days* (1954) by Julian Slade. Andrew Lloyd Webber kept London stocked with musicals for the last three decades of the twentieth century.

From the 1950s continental influences made an impact not only on small scale 'intellectual' theatre in Britain but also on university drama groups and the more serious amateur companies. Many of these incursions Martin Esslin, the theatre writer, referred to as the 'Theatre of the Absurd'. Samuel Beckett, some of whose plays were first written in French and received their premieres in Paris, became known here through *Waiting for Godot* (1953) in which audiences were taught much about existentialism through the mouths of Vladimir and Estragon. Some of Beckett's plays held a theatrical appeal but others were over-rarified: a single stationary actress in a thirty minute piece has little hope of making a mark. Eugène Ionesco, son of a Romanian father and a French mother, had a similar introduction to British audiences: plays most often to be found staged in out-of-the-way places were *The Bald Prima Donna* (1950) and *The Lesson* (1951). Of the foreign playwrights it was Bertolt Brecht who made the widest impact on British theatre: *Mother Courage and her Children* was given its first performance in this country in 1955 at Barnstaple and the following year Brecht's troupe of actors, the Berliner Ensemble, brought *The Caucasian Chalk Circle* to the Palace Theatre in the west end. The writings of Antonin Artaud, another

Frenchman, helped drama to break out of the conventional theatre building. Artaud envisaged a drama space as a large hangar in which the audience sat in swivel chairs so the encompassing action could go on at ground level and above along gantries and balconies. The divide between spectators and players was to be broken down and the traditional safety afforded by a typical Edwardian theatre would no longer protect the playgoer from a wholesale onslaught by the cast. Obviously he had an effect on such productions as *Oh, What a Lovely War!* (1963) by Joan Littlewood, the Peter Brook production of *A Midsummer Night's Dream* (1595–6) staged in a Persian circus and the direction by Charles Marowitz of John Herbert's *Fortune and Men's Eyes*, staged in a Tottenham Court Road cellar known as The Open Space, in which each audience 'participant' was subjected to the same treatment – shackles and finger-prints – meted out to criminals.

'I doubt if I could love anyone who did not wish to see *Look Back in Anger*,' wrote Kenneth Tynan in the *Observer* in 1956, 'It is the best young play of its decade.' George Devine's newly formed English Stage Company mounted the play at the small Royal Court Theatre in Sloane Square. Many critics heralded the play as a break through the parameters of drama with an anti-hero, Jimmy Porter, as the 'angry young man' out of key with society and personal relationships. It may have been sordid but was for many a 'slice of life' as they had experienced it and soon this type of drama was to be branded as 'kitchen sink'. Others of the same ilk followed: Shelagh Delaney's *A Taste of Honey* (1958) received its premiere at Stratford East, although it portrayed life in Manchester, and Arnold Wesker's *Roots* (1959), telling of life and culture in Norfolk, opened at the Belgrade Theatre in Coventry before a transfer to Sloane Square. But Wesker's ideal audience would have consisted of 'the bus driver, the housewife, the miner and the Teddy Boy.'[1] Bernard Kops' plays similarly brought Jewish folklore to the stage as in *The Hamlet of Stepney Green* (1956), a comic reading of the Hamlet theme. These writers presented realism with a vengeance but their influence infiltrated outside the theatre as television in consequence became rougher and lost its desire to see urban working-class life through the filters of middle-class respectability. It had to be a first hand experience.

Above all, the proletarian drama was an escape from the trammels of the 'well-made play' format, three acts, at least two of which were set in the drawing room of an affluent household in Loamshire, within which a well-regulated and expected plot was unveiled. Its prime exponents were Terence Rattigan, William Douglas Home and Graham Greene. The latter's earlier novels had demonstrated that he was interested in maintaining a pattern in his writing. In *Stamboul Train* (1932), for example, the progress of the trans-European journey fits the sections of the book. Later, he demonstrated the same skill in the structure of his dramas, although they dug deeper than this as they gradually revealed the ways of man's dealing in his search for God. *The Potting Shed* (1958) in which John Gielgud starred was one of the most acceptable of these and continues to be revived.

By the 1970s a new kind of individualistic playwright was emerging. The massive consumption of both radio and television was an encouragement to inexperienced writers; shorter length plays were less formidable to tackle and flexibility, including the opportunity to work as part of a team on soaps, gave the nervous individual assurance. Because of their lack of common formation and purpose the writers are almost impossible to group but any from the following list composed of playwrights for stage and television are worth perusing: Robert Bolt, Joe Orton, Tom Stoppard, Peter Shaffer, Harold Pinter, Alan Ayckbourn, Charles Wood, John Arden, Alan Plater, David Mercer and Dennis Potter.

To finish this section, a number of tendencies relating to theatre writers may be considered. From the mid-century companies were established which would not only perform plays but also write, or often more accurately evolve, the show with its definable house style. One such company is Shared Experience which has taken such established novels as *A Passage to India* (E M Forster, 1924) and *The Mill on the Floss* (George Eliot, 1860) telling the story through individuals or small groups of actors – sometimes by several actors representing one character – using objects, such as the millrace in which Maggie Tulliver drowns, as icons and regarding much of the novel's material as notes for a highly physical ritual. Similarly one sometimes comes across 'evolved' work involving the cast during the rehearsal period improvising around a number of themes, locations and roles. Whether or not this requires a writer to formalise the dialogue depends on the expectations of the polish of the finished work. The development of *Oh, What a Lovely War!* depended on such an approach and it has sometimes been used since. Novels, especially lengthy classics, have also formed a basis for performance, evolved in the manner outlined above or otherwise stemming from the adaptation of a writer as in the case of Fay Weldon's work on Gustave Flaubert's *Madame Bovary* (1857). Respected plays from the past have also received adaptations. An example on circuit at the time of writing is *Hobson's Choice,* originally written in 1916 by Harold Brighouse, one of the Manchester school of dramatists, and at the beginning of this century recast by Tanika Gupta, set in Salford and peopled by a family of Pakistanis running a clothing factory in place of the boot-makers of the original play.

The changing acting place

The traditional Edwardian theatre, continuing to be the norm in London's west end, whilst suitable for the mid-nineteenth-century box sets of Madame Vestris, offered merely a cramped stage unsuitable for shows involving dance, singing and the provision of an orchestra. One of the proponents of the open stage was Tyrone Guthrie. Asked by the Edinburgh Festival committee to stage Sir David Lyndsay's morality play *The Three Estates* (1540), Guthrie realised that the proscenium arch theatre was completely unsuitable for the purpose: 'Scene after scene seemed absolutely unplayable on the proscenium stage, almost meaningless in terms of "dramatic illusion".'[2] In 1953 Guthrie was appointed one of the directors of the Festival Theatre, Stratford, Ontario where he was influential in securing a thrust stage with audience seating on three sides. He advised on the building of the Festival Theatre at Chichester, a building also with a large open stage with the audience on three sides, a semi-permanent balcony running across the rear of the stage and exits and entrances from two ramps in the auditorium on either side of the stage and further doorways leading direct from stage to wings. Other new theatres and alterations have been on a smaller scale. Bernard Miles built a new theatre, the Mermaid, at Puddle Dock in a disused warehouse; the end-stage was plain and unencumbered by a proscenium arch or front tabs. Numbers of repertory theatres have had new buildings, one of the most notable of which is The Rep in Broad Street, Birmingham, with a cliffhanger auditorium and a spacious open stage. Numbers of secondary and drama schools have been provided with valuable studio theatres built into a large room hung with black drapes and equipped with bleaches providing stepped seating which may be used in a variety of formations, thus offering great flexibility for productions. Some historic buildings, such as the Lyceum in Sheffield and the Theatre Royal in Nottingham, have benefited from an archaeological restoration after which they gleam in colour and gold leaf.

Playwrights: initiators of new ideas in the theatre

William Butler Yeats

Thirty years before Brecht was considering how his polemical plays might be presented, William Butler Yeats was traversing the same ground, considering the possibilities for his own plays as well as those of his fellow-writer John Millington Synge. The principles on which the Irishman and the German worked were much the same with simplicity and stillness as important conventions. Yeats noted:

> It was certainly a day of triumph when the first act of *The Well of the Saints* held its audience though the two chief persons sat side by side under a stone cross from start to finish...The players still try to preserve [stillness], though audiences accustomed to the cinema expect constant change...[3]

Yeats went on to complain that convention demanded that speakers of soliloquies should always face the audience and stand far apart from each other. Finally, in stating the conventions within which he would have his plays performed, the playwright wrote of the importance of the spoken word:

> I had begun to get rid of everything that is not, whether in lyric or dramatic poetry, in some sense character in action; a pause in the midst of action perhaps, but action always its end and theme.

Of course, the plot dictates the method of staging and again there is a similarity between the folk tales of Brecht and the fairy ramblings of Yeats. In *The Countess Cathleen* (1892), the scene is laid at an indeterminate time, but one ravaged by famine and the country people sell their souls to demons for food in spite of the alleviation the Countess makes for them. A judgement is called for from the audience when she sells her own soul in order to help her people, just as the German audience had continually to make moral evaluations on the predicaments of Brecht's characters, such as Mother Courage.

Bertolt Brecht

One of the direct influences on Bertolt Brecht was Erwin Piscator, a German theatre director whose productions were on an epic scale, breaking down the traditional Aristotelian 'unities' of time and place; they seemed as irrelevant as they would in a Shakespeare play as the audience travelled from Rome to Egypt in *Antony and Cleopatra* (1606–7) or from Belmont to the Venetian canals in *The Merchant of Venice* (1596–8). Ironically Brecht was a playwright who failed in his professional life to compose a plot, taking instead Biblical episodes, folk tales, biographies or existing entertainments such as *The Beggar's Opera* (1728) which he revamped as *The Threepenny Opera* using it as a means of furthering the communist dialectic. However, the ideas behind Brecht's methods of production hold more interest than the narrative lines of his presentations and these may be studied in the work of the Berliner Ensemble, a company he founded in East Berlin in 1949. Unlike Stanislavsky who, when rehearsing the performers of the Moscow Arts Theatre, stressed the importance of identification with one's role, Brecht demanded of his actors a distancing from their roles, partly that members of the audience might exercise a critical faculty and make judgements on the argument presented, summarising them within their own conclusions about the ideology presented within the play. However, it is unwise to be over-dictatorial about his methodology: Brecht himself varied his theory to suit the practicalities of staging and indeed his most creative plays allow for a variety of technical approaches.

Brecht stripped down the stage so that it resembles an unlocalised *platea*, with some similarities to the Elizabethan stage. On it one meets the same few properties and suggestions of scenery representing the technology Brecht grew up with. Many of his plays require a large screen on which rhymes may be projected either at the start or end of an episode forming an introduction or a considered judgement of the situation. Often the words are sung by a character with an accompaniment provided by a few instruments. Lowered flats are sometimes used to restrict the acting space and give a feel of intimacy; at other times a long rope is strung across the acting area allowing a curtain – only six or seven feet high – to be drawn so that a scene or pageant may be set behind. Flown iconic motifs have their uses, suggesting either a location or an ideology. One of the simplest but most effective suggestions of location in *The Caucasian Chalk Circle* (1948) is the river separating Grusha from her lover, made from a long blue cloth over which the two young people call messages.

After Brecht's death the Ensemble was directed by his widow, Helen Weigel, who used her husband's presentational ideas with several English plays including the unlikely choice of those of Bernard Shaw. However, it is obvious that Littlewood's *Oh, What a Lovely War!* with its comments and judgements and incongruity of a troupe of pierrots presenting a show about the carnage of war can be traced to the influence of Brecht as well as many 'evolved' productions.

Samuel Beckett

Samuel Beckett is the authority on time passing. Born in Dublin, he did most of his writing – the range is wide, consisting of plays, novels, poetry, criticisms – in French, declaring that to write in an acquired language makes it easier to write without style. In both French and English his play *Waiting for Godot* (1955) attracted enormous attention in spite of puzzling his early audiences. Such plot as there is consists of two men, neither young nor smart, sitting beneath a tree, attempting to get time to pass whilst they wait for the appearance of Godot, a name of French extraction referring to a 'little God'. They enact various vaudeville and cross talk routines, planning such activities as hanging themselves from the tree. It is only when Lucky and Pozzo appear – in the absence of direct information the audience feels that they may be a cottager and a member of the Ascendancy – do they realise that they can be entertained by external events:

> Vladimir: Charming evening we're having.
> Estragon: Unforgettable.
> Vladimir: And it's not over.
> Estragon: Apparently not.
> Vladimir: It's only beginning.
> Estragon: It's awful.
> Vladimir: Worse than the pantomime.
> Estragon: The circus.
> Vladimir: The music-hall.
> Estragon: The circus.

But there is more to this world than first appears, for the tree and indeed the two vagrants (if that is what they are) are clothed with symbolism. In the Garden of Eden grew the Tree of the Knowledge of Good and Evil and this one seems to be a scion cut from it. It also exemplifies the conceit found in mediaeval illuminated manuscripts: that the wood of the cross on which Christ was crucified grows from the Eden tree. Damnation and salvation have the same cure at root. When the audience returns to the auditorium after the interval Beckett has a further puzzle, for the tree has grown four or five leaves and one asks whether he had in mind the line by Dante in the *Purgatorio*: 'The tree renewed itself which before had its boughs so naked.'

The names of the two tramps suggest that they are archetypes: Estragon, named after the tarragon herb, seems to be Gallic and Vladimir perhaps originates from Russia. What we know for certain is that Estragon suffers from foot trouble, his boots never fit him, and Vladimir has stinking breath and his head is the wrong shape for many of the hats he tries on. We are less sure whether Estragon is an earthy character whose passions are disordered (the signs of this are the saved and damned foot dividing his personality) or whether his partner is possessed by delusions of the mind. Some critics have seen further into the symbol of the two feet: they represent the two thieves on the cross of whom one is saved when he acknowledges his need whilst the self-possessed malefactor is damned. Beckett makes occasional cross-references to the writings of Saint Augustine of Hippo throughout the play and here we are reminded of his dictum that of the two thieves one was saved that none might despair but only one so that none might presume.

The principal theme of the play is not 'Who is Godot?' – if Beckett had known that answer he would have written it into the play – nor yet whether Godot will eventually arrive. Instead we are in the theatre waiting, just as the characters are waiting too, for both audience (its personnel are referred to as 'inspiring prospects') and cast share the same time scale; this is what the play is 'about'.

A further play, *Krapp's Last Tape* (1958), is also concerned with time and waiting. The aged Krapp records on each birthday a summary of the year that has elapsed and then listens to his former memories. Krapp's earlier self seems to be a stranger to his present one and he is reduced to looking up some words from his journal in the dictionary. This is a bleak existence, redeemed only by a lyrical interlude in which a scene on the lake is retrieved from the recesses of memory. Perhaps Estragon has jettisoned Vladimir for technology, hoping that the recaptured past will lead him to salvation.

Margaret Drabble has suggested that three playwrights have been deeply influenced by Beckett; they are Harold Pinter, Athol Fugard and Tom Stoppard.[4]

John Osborne

Had John Osborne not written *Look Back in Anger* (1956), it is doubtful he would have appeared in a list of theatrical innovators. The shape of the work resembles the well-made-plays of two French farceurs of the nineteenth century, Scribe and Sardou, in which repetitions of the stage picture reinforce the dialogue. The obvious patterning in *Anger* is the similar stage arrangement for acts one and three showing Porter complete with newspaper and the current *amour* doing the ironing. However, in *Anger* attention is captured by the characters and the language they use. Strangely, in the case of Jimmy Porter this is not the language of a depressed section of the Midlands's population but ideas framed into a coherent and fluent argument. Speaking of Alison, his wife, he says:

> Living day and night with another human being has made me predatory and suspicious. I know that the only way of finding out exactly what's going on is to catch them when they don't know you're looking. When she goes out, I go through everything. Why?

To see if there is something of me somewhere, a
reference to me.

John Russell Taylor finds for the most part that Porter, as
written, speaks the language of petulance rather than anger
and that the initiator of the stage role, Kenneth Haigh, and
the film role, Richard Burton, present their characters as
heroic figures with an absence of neuroses.[5] Here is the
atmos-phere of life in the post world war urban area, an
atmosphere that provided fodder for the books of novelists
but until this time had been absent in theatrical presentations.

Instead of breaking new ground, both *The Entertainer*
(1957) and *Luther* (1961) were reliant on the type of
organisation and staging Brecht employed in his plays. In the
first of these Osborne takes a fading – and perhaps never
very good – music hall comedian and tracks his professional
demise whilst the second not only relies on Brecht for shape
but for stretches of the dialogue on the American
psychologist with an interest in Martin Luther, Eric Ericsson.
However, Brecht has the ability when presenting a historical
personage simultaneously to teach and to be entertaining, as
his reconstruction of the ideas of Galileo shows in the play
of the same name (1947) but in *Luther* the didactic element
holds up the play. Another which worked well in the theatre
was his historical drama *A Patriot for Me* (1965), showing
the decline of an officer in the Austro-Hungarian army
under the impact of his homosexuality. It was one of the few
pieces to get past the barriers of respectability normally
protecting the Festival Theatre in Chichester and the
Haymarket in London, both in 1983.

Certainly an experimenter, Osborne moved through a
number of dramatic genres and his early death in 1994
prevented him rediscovering the success of *Look Back in
Anger*.

Harold Pinter

Harold Pinter grew up in the East End of London and attended Hackney Downs Grammar School. As a Jewish child he became aware that it was necessary to ward off fascist abuse from his peers with language that could attack as well as parry and communicate. Once he began work on the stage he learned 'how actorly responses', in Simon Trussler's words, 'can lend some dignity even to mediocre fare and be trusted with the moments between the words when richer material allows'.[6] There was considerable interest in the 1960s, when Pinter began to write plays, in 'the space between words', the silence which emphasises possible differences between the transmission and reception of the spoken idea. This philosophical concept Pinter brought to the stage, both in his writing and also in directing, with consummate skill.

Among the characteristics of the conventions he adopts in his early writing is the use of a peopled room, from which characters look out onto an urban landscape seemingly unfriendly. In *The Dumb Waiter* (1958) a serving lift descends with strange orders for meals written on scraps of paper and it becomes the aim of the two hit-men whose living room is the former kitchen of the café to provide at least recognisable substitutes. One feels dangerous presences in *The Birthday Party* (1958), which considers the role of uninvited guests as two of them come to Stanley's celebration. Pinter's name was made by *The Caretaker* (1960), this time set in a claustrophobic house in which the tramp interloper Davies attempts to prise a rift between Aston and Mick, two brothers with a strong inter-dependence. Atypically it is Aston, one of the supporting characters, who shelters within the house, or earlier in a mental hospital, for Davies seems to have the run of the home counties searching for a pair of comfortable shoes.

At the time of writing *The Caretaker*, and developing this further in *The Homecoming* (1965), Pinter experiments with the problem of reality. Can statements and assertions be taken at face value or are they merely part of the self-creating inner world of the speaker? *Betrayal* (1978), a triangle drama, presents the audience with two close friends and a woman who may or may not combine the roles of wife and mistress. Intriguingly the play begins at the end of the affair, working backwards to the seminal encounter. Although Pinter is a prolific writer, this selection of a few early works indicates growing areas of experiment and the fascination with that state which many of the audience accept too easily as 'reality'.

Some poets of the twentieth century

The first world war (1914–8) prompted some of the most distinguished poetry writing of the century. Much of this was composed in conditions of combat in which Wilfred Owen, Edmund Blunden and Charles Hamilton Sorley gave horrifyingly realistic descriptions of the carnage, a counterbalance to the romantic view of battle exemplified in the poems of Rupert Brooke.

In addition to writing plays in verse and prose John Masefield's output of poetry was prodigious, beginning with a nostalgic regard for his early seafaring life and progressing to some complete long works such as *Reynard the Fox* (1919), a graphic description of a hunt, and *The Everlasting Mercy* (1911), a controversial work in which colloquial language, sometimes blasphemous, was used. He formed a friendship with W B Yeats paying tribute to him in *Some Memories of W B Yeats* (1940). In 1930 he succeeded Robert Bridges as Poet Laureate and was awarded the Order of Merit five years later.

One of the most significant writers of the twentieth century is also one of the strangest; she is Dame Edith

Sitwell whose interest in Modernism shaped her poetry into a sharp contrast with that of, say, Masefield who throughout his life remained in the Georgian mould. Modernism, strong on novelty, flourished in the first half of the century opening the gates of poetry and the novel to experimentation with such techniques as the 'stream of consciousness' a device used by Virginia Woolf in *To the Lighthouse* (1927). At the Chenil Gallery in Chelsea Sitwell spoke her suite of poems, *Façade*, through a megaphone hidden behind a sheet on which a face and open mouth were painted, to music written by William Walton. The words, sometimes indiscernible, concentrated on sounds and syncopated rhythms giving the impression of a tale for children:

Lily O'Grady,
Silly and shady,
Longing to be
A lazy lady,
Walked by the cupolas, gables in the
Lake's Georgian stables...

One of her most telling poems of the second world war is 'Still Falls the Rain' in which the German bombs are compared to a rainstorm; images hark back to the cruel aspects of the Elizabethan world, especially such pastimes as bear-baiting and hare coursing.

For his part Thomas Stearns Eliot was influenced by the Symbolists, a French movement of the previous century whose chief apologist was Stephane Mallarmé. It was the business of a poet – for Mallarmé – 'to paint not the thing but the effect it produces', to some extent the practice of W B Yeats. Even though literary criticism and journalism (he wrote for the *Athenaeum*, *The Times Literary Supplement* and *Dial*) robbed him of time to produce a wide poetic output, the denseness of some of his poems makes them fascinating to unravel as in the 'Four Quartets' and 'The Waste Land'. Some poems, though, are easily accessible among which may be numbered 'The Coming of the Magi', 'The Hippopotamus' and the various pieces in *Old Possum's Book of Practical Cats* (1939) on which the musical *Cats* was based. For Eliot an important point in his life was his reception into the Anglican church in 1927, marked by an increasing optimism in his poetry.

Philip Larkin was an ordinary man, living a very ordinary life: he was in charge of the Brynmor Jones Library at the University of Hull. The major part of his poetry was written after the second world war and demonstrated the disillusion that confronted many people returning to an uneventful working life after service in the forces or armaments factory. The England of pre-war days seemed to have disappeared – 'Church Going' expresses the changing face of the country – and yet sometimes Larkin sums up in a few lines the sheer satisfactoriness of life, as in the minute 'Days':

> What are days for?
> Days are where we live.
> They come, they wake us
> Time and time over. They are to be happy in:
> Where can we live but days?

Two poets influenced Larkin, although his own work was far from resembling theirs; they were W B Yeats and Thomas Hardy. Alongside poetry, another great love in his life was jazz and he regularly reviewed records for the *Daily Telegraph*.

Appropriately, as Larkin warmly admired John Betjeman, he follows him here. A blank verse autobiography, *Summoned by Bells* (1962), gives details of Betjeman's early life and his formation at Magdalen College, Oxford, although he left without a degree. Enthusiasm rather than erudition found him a place amongst the *Architectural Review* writers, a useful placing as many of the studies offered subjects for poems, the first collection of which, *Mount Zion*, was published in 1932. Soon Betjeman had established himself as a topographical poet recording such treasures as Cornish fishing villages, Victorian architecture and Metroland, the stretches of countryside that could be reached by London Transport's northward bound suburban line. He has the power to evoke in a couple of verses a way of life, usually one fast disappearing, in such poems as 'Death in Leamington Spa', 'Pot-Pourri from a Surrey Garden' and the adulatory pieces in honour of Miss Joan Hunter Dunne and her tennis equipment. It is glaringly apparent that Betjeman has models and one can spot the influence of *Hymns Ancient and Modern*, the ubiquitous Thomas Hardy, Parson Hawker of Morwenstow and Alfred Lord Tennyson. In 1972 he succeeded C Day Lewis as Poet Laureate.

Finally another Poet Laureate, Andrew Motion. He taught creative writing at the University of East Anglia and also edited the *Poetry Review*. Motion's poems cover a wide range of subjects and a narrative line is hinted at in many of them. He wrote a distinguished biography of Philip Larkin whom he knew when he lectured at Hull and possibly arising from this is his elegy for him, 'This is your Subject Speaking'. He has also written a book on the poems of Edward Thomas. Nearer home is his close attachment to his mother who died after a long illness, some of which was spent in a coma. Affection speaks clearly through the lines of 'In the Attic' in which he gets out his mother's clothes from the trunk where they are stored, remembering the occasions when they were worn:

> My hands push down between
> hollow, invisible sleeves,

hesitate, then lift
patterns of memory:

a green holiday, a red christening,
all your unfinished lives
fading through dark summers,
entering my head as dust.

Adept at capturing voices, Andrew Motion has used historical characters as the basis for some of his verse: one such is the poem written after visiting Anne Frank's house in Amsterdam. At other times the fresh tones of the authorial 'I' take over: 'I'm awake to a thrush / doodling with its voice…' Throughout the range of subjects one gets the impression that here is a man who questions and challenges.

2. SELECTED AUTHORS, PLAYWRIGHTS AND WORKS OF THE TWENTIETH CENTURY (BRITISH)

Note: Plays are identified by an asterisk preceding the title.

1902: *The Times Literary Supplement* founded

1902: The Hound of the Baskervilles by A Conan Doyle

1904: The Abbey Theatre, Dublin opens

1904: *Riders to the Sea by J M Synge

1906: *The Man of Property by John Galsworthy

1907: Father and Son by Edmund Gosse

1910: Howard's End by E M Forster

1910: *The Madras House by Harley Granville-Barker

1912: *Hindle Wakes by Stanley Houghton

1913: Sons and Lovers by D H Lawrence

1914: First world war begins

1914: *Pygmalion by Bernard Shaw

1915: *Hobson's Choice by Harold Brighouse

1915: The Rainbow by D H Lawrence

1918:   Allied victory and end of the first world war

1918:   Poems by Gerard Manley Hopkins

1921:   British Broadcasting Corporation founded

1922:   Surrealism flourishes (1922–40)

1922:   Ulysses by James Joyce

1922:   Façade by Edith Sitwell

1923:   *Shadow of a Gunman by Sean O'Casey

1923:   *St Joan by Bernard Shaw

1924:   A Passage to India by E M Forster

1924:   *Juno and the Paycock by Sean O'Casey

1925:   Bernard Shaw receives the Nobel Prize for Literature

1925:   *Hay Fever by Noël Coward

1927:   To the Lighthouse by Virginia Woolf

1928:   First television transmission

1928:   Women gain suffrage

1930:   Rise of Nazism in Germany

1930:   Poems by W H Auden

1930:   *Private Lives by Noël Coward

1930:   Vile Bodies by Evelyn Waugh

1932:   John Galsworthy awarded Nobel Prize for Literature

1932:   Stamboul Train by Graham Greene

1932:   Lady Chatterley's Lover, expurgated version by D H Lawrence

1933:   Adolf Hitler appointed German Chancellor

1933:   *Richard of Bordeaux by Gordon Daviot (aka Elizabeth Mackintosh and Josephine Tay)

1935:   *Murder in the Cathedral by T S Eliot

1936:   Death of George V; succeeded by Edward VIII

1936:   *The Ascent of F6 by W H Auden and Christopher Isherwood

1937: Abdication of Edward VIII. Duke of York accedes as George VI

1937: *Time and the Conways by J B Priestley

1937: The Hobbit by J R R Tolkien

1939: Second world war begins

1939: *The Family Reunion by T S Eliot

1941: *Blithe Spirit by Noël Coward

1945: Atomic bomb dropped on Hiroshima and Nagasaki

1945: Brideshead Revisited by Evelyn Waugh

1946: *An Inspector Calls by J B Priestley

1946: *The Winslow Boy by Terence Rattigan

1947: India granted independence by Great Britain

1948: *The Lady's Not for Burning by Christopher Fry

1950: Theatre of the Absurd flourishes until *c.* 1963

1950: The Third Man by Graham Greene

1950: The Lion, the Witch and the Wardrobe by C S Lewis

1952: Death of George VI; accession of Queen Elizabeth II

1954: *Under Milk Wood by Dylan Thomas

1955: *The Chalk Garden by Enid Bagnold

1956: *Look Back in Anger by John Osborne

1957: *Endgame by Samuel Beckett

1957: *The Room by Harold Pinter

1957: *The Entertainer by John Osborne

1958: *The Birthday Party by Harold Pinter

1958: *Five Finger Exercise by Peter Shaffer

1958: *Chicken Soup with Barley by Arnold Wesker

1959: *Serjeant Musgrave's Dance by John Arden

1959: *Roots by Arnold Wesker

1960: *The Caretaker by Harold Pinter

1961: The Prime of Miss Jean Brodie by Muriel Spark

1964: *Entertaining Mr Sloane by Joe Orton

1964: *The Royal Hunt of the Sun by Peter Shaffer

1966: *Rosencrantz and Guildenstern are Dead by Tom Stoppard

> 1968: Cecil Day-Lewis appointed Poet Laureate
>
> 1971: Foundation of the Open University

1971: Maurice by E M Forster

1973: *Bingo by Edward Bond

1973: *Equus by Peter Shaffer

1975: *Fanshen by David Hare

1975: *Comedians by Trevor Griffiths

> 1976: National Theatre opens on South Bank
>
> 1979: Margaret Thatcher becomes first female Prime Minister
>
> 1982: The Falklands War

1982: *Noises Off by Michael Frayn

> 1984: AIDS virus identified

1984: Hotel du Lac by Anita Brookner

1986: Making Cocoa for Kingsley Amis by Wendy Cope

1988: Collected Poems by John Heath Stubbs

1988: *Our Country's Good by Timberlake Wertenbaker

1990: Possession by A S Byatt

1990: *Racing Demon by David Hare

1993: Paddy Clark Ha Ha Ha by Roddy Doyle

1993: *Arcadia by Tom Stoppard

1993: Collected Poems by R S Thomas

1994: The Annals of Chile by Paul Muldoon

1998: *Copenhagen by Michael Frayn

3. BIBLIOGRAPHY

General works

Barnes, Philip, *A Companion to Post-War British Theatre.* Totowa, New Jersey: Barnes and Noble Books, 1986.

Beauman, Sally, *The Royal Shakespeare Company: A History of Ten Decades.* London: Oxford University Press, 1982.

Brook, Peter, *The Empty Space.* Harmondsworth: Penguin, 1972.

Esslin, Martin, *The Theatre of the Absurd,* 3rd edition. Harmondsworth: Penguin, 1983.

Hinchliffe, Arnold P, *Modern Verse Drama.* London: Methuen, The Critical Idiom no. 32, 1977.

Joseph, Stephen, *Theatre in the Round.* London: Barrie and Rockcliffe, 1967.

Marshall, Norman, *The Other Theatre.* London: Theatre Book Club, 1950.

The National Theatre: Special Issue in *Gambit,* vol 7, no 28, 1976.

Robinson, Lennox, *Ireland's Abbey Theatre: A History, 1899–1951.* London: Sidgwick and Jackson, 1951.

Williams, Raymond, *Drama from Ibsen to Eliot.* Harmondsworth: Penguin Books Ltd, 1964.

Playwrights and other writers: biography, criticism and collected works

John Arden

Gray, Francis, *John Arden.* London: Macmillan, Macmillan Modern Drama Lists, 1982.

Hunt, Albert, *Arden: A Study of his Plays.* London: Eyre Methuen, 1974.

Alan Ayckbourn

Watson, Ian, *Conversations with Ayckbourn.* London: Macdonald, 1981.

Samuel Beckett

Blair, Deirdre, *Samuel Beckett: A Biography*. London: Picador, 1978.

Coe, Richard N, *Beckett*. Edinburgh: Oliver and Boyd Ltd, Writers and Critics, 1964.

Kenner, Hugh, *A Reader's Guide to Samuel Beckett*. London: Thames and Hudson, 1973.

Bertolt Brecht

Morley, Michael, *Brecht: A Study*. London: Heinemann, 1977.

Willett, John, *The Theatre of Bertolt Brecht*. London: Eyre Methuen, rev. 1977.

Caryl Churchill

Truss Lynn, 'A Fair Cop', in *Plays and Players*, January 1984.

Noël Coward

Hoare, Philip, *Noël Coward. A Biography*. London: Sinclair-Stevenson, 1993.

Lahr, John, *Coward the Playwright*. London: Methuen, 1982.

T S Eliot

Browne, E Martin, *The Making of T S Eliot's Plays*. Cambridge: Cambridge University Press, 1970.

John Galsworthy

Barker, D, *The Man of Principle: A View of John Galsworthy*. London: Allen and Unwin, 1963.

Harley Granville-Barker

Kennedy D, *Granville-Barker and the Dream of Theatre*. Cambridge: Cambridge University Press, 1985.

Graham Greene

Spurling, John, *Graham Greene*. London: Methuen, Contemporary Writers, 1983.

Tyrone Guthrie

Guthrie, Tyrone, *A Life in the Theatre*. London: Columbus Books, 1987.

John Osborne

Hinchliffe, Arnold P, 'Whatever Happened to John Osborne?' in *Contemporary English Drama* ed. C W E Bigsby. London: Edward Arnold, 1981.

Osborne, John, *A Better Class of Person*. Harmondsworth: Penguin, 1982.

Harold Pinter

Esslin, Martin, *The Peopled Wound*. London: Methuen and Co Ltd, 1970.

Esslin, Martin, *Pinter: A Study of his Plays*. London: Eyre Methuen, 1973.

Hayman, Ronald, *Harold Pinter*. London: Heinemann, 1976.

Peter Shaffer

Russell Taylor, John, *Peter Shaffer*. London: Longman and the British Council, Writers and their Work, 1974.

J M Synge

Strong L A G, *John Millington Synge*. London: Allen and Unwin, 1941.

George Bernard Shaw

Weintraub, S, *The Unexpected Shaw: Biographical approaches to GBS and his work*. New York: P Ungar, 1982.

Ward A C, *Bernard Shaw*. London: published for the British Council by Longmans, Green and Co [1951].

Tom Stoppard

Hayman, Ronald, *Tom Stoppard*. London: Heinemann Educational Books, 4th edition, 1982.

William Butler Yeats

Jeffares, A Norman and Knowland, A S, *A Commentary on the Collected Plays of W B Yeats*. Stanford, USA: Stanford University Press, 1975.

Jeffares, A Norman, *W B Yeats: Man and Poet*. Dublin: Gill and Macmillan, 1996.

Biographies of actors, designers and other theatre professionals

Peter Brook

Trewin, J C, *Peter Brook: A Biography*. London: Macmillan, 1971.

Edith Evans

Forbes, Bryan, *Dame Edith Evans: Ned's Girl*. Boston and Toronto: Little, Brown and Co, 1977.

John Gielgud

Gielgud, John, *An Actor in his Time*. Harmondsworth: Penguin, 1979.

Alec Guinness

Guinness, Alec, *Blessings in Disguise*. London: Hamish Hamilton, 1985.

Taylor, John Russell, *Alec Guinness: A Celebration*. London: Pavilion Books, 1983.

Tyrone Guthrie

Forsyth, James, *Tyrone Guthrie: A Biography*. London: Hamish Hamilton, 1975.

Guthrie, Tyrone, *A Life in the Theatre*. London: Hamish Hamilton, 1960.

Michael Hordern

Hordern, Michael and Edwards, Christopher, 'Parts Ancient and Modern', *Plays and Players*, May 1983.

Ann Jellicoe

Jellicoe, Ann, *Some Unconscious Influences in the Theatre*. London: Cambridge University Press, 1967.

Mike Leigh

Clements, Paul, *The Improvised Play: The Work of Mike Leigh*. London: Methuen, Methuen Theatrefile, 1983.

Charles Marowitz

Marowitz, Charles, *The Act of Being*. London: Secker and Warburg, 1978.

Anthony Sher

Sher, Anthony, *The Year of the King*. London: Chatto and Windus, 1983.

Sybil Thorndike

Morley, Sheridan, *Sybil Thorndike: A Life in the Theatre*. London: Weidenfeld and Nicolson, 1977.

Timothy West

West, Timothy, *A moment towards the end of the play...* London: Nick Hern Books, 2002.

Books on poets and poetry

John Betjeman

Brown, Dennis, *John Betjeman*. Plymouth: Northcote House in association with the British Council, Writers and their Work, 1999.

Hillier, Bevis, *Young Betjeman*. London: Cardinal, 1988.

T S Eliot

Blamires, Harry, *Word Unheard: A Guide through Eliot's Four Quartets*. London: Methuen and Co Ltd, 1969.

Kenner, H, *The Invisible Poet: Thomas Stearnes Eliot*. London: Methuen, 1974.

Philip Larkin

Motion, Andrew, *Philip Larkin*. London: Routledge, 1988.

Thwaite, Anthony, ed, *Collected Poems of Philip Larkin*. London: Faber, 2003.

Thwaite, Anthony, ed, *Selected Letters of Philip Larkin; 1940–1985*. London: Faber,1992.

John Masefield

Spark, Muriel, *John Masefield*. London: Hutchinson, 1992.

Andrew Motion

Hulse, M, ' "I Could Have Outlived Myself There": the Poetry of Andrew Motion' in *Critical Quarterly*, 28 (1986), 71–81.

Wilfred Owen

Hibberd, Dominic, *Wilfred Owen: A New Biography*. London:
    Weidenfeld and Nicolson, 1992.

Sitwell family

Cevasco, G A, *The Sitwells, Edith, Osbert and Sacheverell*.
    Boston, Mass: Twayne, 1987.

Anthologies of poetry

Gardner, Brian, ed, *Up the Line to Death*. London: Methuen,
    1986.

Stallworthy, Jon, ed, *The Oxford Book of War Poetry*. Oxford:
    Oxford University Press, 1984.

The social background

Fraser, G S, *The Modern Writer and his World*. Harmondsworth:
    Penguin, 1953.

Manvell, Roger, *The Film and the Public*. Harmondsworth:
    Penguin, 1955.

4.   SOME POINTS FOR DISCUSSION

- Could the movement for realism in the theatre
  be justified? Consider some of its advocates
  and give examples of the attempted use of
  realism.

- The repertory system: would it work in the
  current provincial or London theatre?

- What advantages, if any, has the verse drama
  over the naturalistic play, both of the past and
  contemporary?

- Is the term 'Theatre of the Absurd' a misnomer
  when applied to the plays of Samuel Beckett?

- Do some of the poets of the second half of
  the twentieth century hold a common vision?

- Have the changes in the shape of the acting area over the last one hundred years altered playwrights' approaches to their craft?

5.   NOTES AND REFERENCES

1   From an essay by Arnold Wesker under the title 'Let Battle Commence' and cited in Philip Barnes, *A Companion to Post-War British Theatre*. Totowa, New Jersey: Barnes and Noble Books, 1986, p 254.

2   Tyrone Guthrie, *A Life in the Theatre*. London: Columbus Books, 1987, p 275.

3   W B Yeats, 'An Introduction for my Plays' (1937) cited in *The Collected Works of W B Yeats, Volume II: The Plays*, ed David R and Rosalind E Clark. Basingstoke: Palgrave, 2001.

4   Margaret Drabble, *The Concise Oxford Companion to English Literature*, ed Margaret Drabble and Jenny Stringer. Oxford: Oxford University Press, 1990, p 43.

5   John Russell Taylor, *Anger and After*. Harmondsworth: Penguin Books, p 42.

6   Simon Trussler, entry on Harold Pinter, *The Continuum Encyclopedia of British Literature*, ed Steven R Serafin and Wendy Grosvenor Myer. New York and London: Continuum International Publishing Group, 2003, p 764.

TWENTIETH-CENTURY
AMERICAN DRAMA

1. SURVEY

The business of adaptation

Unlike the British writer who tends to specialise in a single literary genre such as poetry, the novel, playwriting, essays or biography, the American writer tends to cast his net wider and gets to grips with a number of different forms. Thus plays may be written by someone who is equally at home when transferring his skill to romantic novels and poetry. Perhaps it is this breadth of appreciation that is responsible for the American playwright's ability to hand over his script to those who specialise in musical comedy or song and dance shows, so that a text rapidly makes its way through a number of modes until the original narrative line, or the tone of the original piece may be barely discernable. As an example one may look at a novel for children written in 1900 by L Frank Baum, *The Wonderful Wizard of Oz*, which enjoyed several adaptations. The writer was born outside Syracuse, NY, in 1856 and was raised in a small community. As a teenager he quickly mastered the requirements of journalism but decided in his maturity to write a fairy story for the young, different in kind from the ones he had read as an infant in which terror was often an integral part. The book was successful to the extent that the author turned it into a musical for adults, first staged in 1902. In turn, this was translated into a Technicolor film in 1939 with Judy Garland playing the principal role of Dorothy. A far cry from this movie was *The Wiz*, a musical with a black cast that used a modern urban setting and opened on Broadway in 1975.

Some noted American playwrights of the twentieth century

Eugene O'Neill, realism and expressionism

Almost as if Eugene O'Neill were gathering experiences that he could later use in his plays, his early life consisted of stints as a gold prospector, beachcomber, fisherman, vagrant and actor. His earliest stage writing was in conjunction with the Provincetown Players where he practiced a form of realism illustrated in *Anna Christie* (1921), the story of the gradual redemption of a prostitute. Alongside this, he also experimented with expressionism seen in two of his lasting plays, *The Emperor Jones (1920)* and *The Hairy Ape* (1922). In the latter the brutal protagonist Yank is shown as an isolate living in a society yoked to the machine. The two terms used above need some explanation: in the history of art, realism refers usually to the nineteenth-century painter Courbet and reflects a new interest in the ordinary and everyday. There are parallels with this idea in the theatre but it has to be said that the heroes and heroines of the stage are often forced by life's circumstances to come to terms with the limitations of possibility. Expressionism on the other hand began as a painters' movement (Vincent Van Gogh and Edvard Munch may be seen as its precursors) and spread to the theatre and cinema where inner feelings were expressed overtly with passion through heightening and distorting image and behaviour. The writings of Jung and Freud were studied and theatrically applied. With his deepening skill, O'Neill became interested in Aeschylus's trilogy of plays, *The Oresteia* (458 BC), which in *Mourning Becomes Electra* (1931) he shifted to America at the end of the Civil War, recounting his narrative through the Mannon family. *Long Day's Journey into Night* (1956) was published and presented posthumously and is arguably his greatest work, again a family-based epic built around a retired actor, James Tyrone and his wife Mary who at the start of the play has recently returned home from a clinic at which she was being treated for drug addiction. Partly autobiographical, the play was described during the writing by O'Neill as a 'play of old sorrow, written in tears and blood'.

The Little Theatre movement

O'Neill's output beds in with a couple of the New York theatre movements. From 1910 theatres outside New York that had previously booked touring companies were changing to showing silent films, an entertainment for the whole family, complete with action and slapstick. Seats were cheaper than they had been under the former regime. Eschewing celluloid, the Little Theatre movement, sometimes presented by amateurs, was anti-commercial with a European consciousness that favoured the plays of Ibsen, Shaw and Chekhov. But Provincetown was distinctive. It was a small village on the tip of Cape Cod, the summer home of a colony of artists and social reformers. The local players were directed by Maurice Browne, a follower of Edward Gordon Craig, son of the famous British actress Ellen Terry. Performed by the Provincetown Players, O'Neill began to obtain recognition which spread when the company wintered in Greenwich Village, buying its own theatre there where *The Emperor Jones* first brought O'Neill public acclamation. This was extended when his work, seen on the Little Theatre stages, began to be published: there were the *Provincetown Plays* of 1916, some of his sea plays in 1919 and *The Long Voyage Home* in *Smart Set* (1920), a theatre magazine. The more technically demanding of O'Neill's plays were mounted by the Theatre Guild, many of them during the Great Depression of the early 1930s. Theatres affiliated to the Guild later functioned on a subscription basis.

Elmer Rice

A law school graduate turned playwright, Elmer Rice is chiefly remembered for his interest in the structure of a couple of his plays. The first stage work, *On Trial* (1914) was a murder mystery shaped by the ritual of a trial in which the cinematic process of presenting scenes in cutback (flash back) was employed; pace in the narration was helped by the use of a stage revolve. His more renowned work is *The Adding Machine* (1923), an expressionistic play dealing with Mr Zero's attempts to circumvent the dehumanising effect of mechanisation. In this, too, movie-editing technique was adopted.

Thornton Wilder

'Wilder is perpetually aflame with ideas,' wrote Kenneth Tynan in the *Observer*, 21 August 1955. Perhaps Wilder was at his happiest when he could weave an arabesque around an established text, a skill which led to charges of plagiarism; thus *The Skin of our Teeth* (1942) is based on *Finnegan's Wake* (1939) by the Irish writer James Joyce and *A Life in the Sun* (1955) finds its root in Euripides' *Alcestis* (438 BC). Even his own work becomes grist for the mill: an unsuccessful comedy *The Merchant of Yonkers* (1939) was rewritten as *The Matchmaker* (1954) and then, discovering the apotheosis of triumph, was presented as *Hello Dolly!* (1964), a musical.

Princeton, New Jersey, and New York were taken by surprise in 1938 with the advent of *Our Town*, an area of Grover's Corners in New Hampshire within which the audience is invited to watch the everyday events of a couple of families and the growing warmth of a relationship between two of their children. The usual comforting opulence of a set was denied the spectators:

No curtain.

No scenery.

The audience, arriving, sees an empty stage in half-light.

Presently the stage manager, hat on and pipe in mouth, enters and begins placing a table and three chairs downstage left, and a table and three chairs downstage right. He also places a low bench at the corner of what will be the Webb house, left.

As the house lights go down he has finished setting the stage and leaning against the right proscenium pillar watches the late arrivals in the audience.

When the auditorium is in complete darkness he speaks.

Commenting on the play before a revival was presented at the Edinburgh Festival in 1955, Tynan wrote:

With a few chairs as scenery and a philosophic Stage Manager as chorus, he evolved the seasonal rhythm of small-town life so perfectly that Grover's Corners, New Hampshire, was placed not only geographically but cosmically: at times one seemed, as Wilder says, 'to be looking at the town through the wrong end of a lunar telescope.' Like Turgenev, he hit his full stride as the scholar-poet of provincial life.

When tackled about the staging, Wilder referred to Molière's dictum that all the theatre required was 'a platform and a passion or two'.

Ben Hecht

As the twenties gave way to the thirties several playwrights were remembered not by their complete *oeuvre* but by a single presentation. This is true of Hecht, Connelly and Riggs. Ben Hecht came from Wisconsin to Chicago after the first world war (1914–18), plunging into its literary world with the editorship of the *Chicago Literary Times*, one of a number of 'little magazines', numbering over three hundred in the States, one of which had given a fillip to the writing of James Joyce by printing advance excerpts in the *Egoist* from *A Portrait of the Artist as a Young Man*, to mention just one instance of their virtue. Taken with play writing, a vast output followed but the best known of his works in this genre, written in conjunction with Charles MacArthur, is *The Front Page* (1928) dealing with the Chicago newsmen and the madhouse on Madison Street together with the narrative line of the stamping down of a young reporter by his editor. The play was adapted for the screen on a number of occasions; the most famous version was *His Girl Friday* (1940) with Cary Grant and Rosalind Russell followed by versions directed by Billy Wilder (1974) and Ted Kotcheff (1988).

Marc Connelly

Connelly's play *Merton of the Movies* (1922) is now forgotten but not *The Green Pastures* (1930). This is a version of Roark Bradford's adaptation of biblical stories, Afro-American in conception, covering episodes from Creation to the Crucifixion as if presented as a series of tableaux in a Southern black church. Six years later Connelly adapted the play as a film with an all-black cast, a production receiving mixed notices. About it, the black film historian Donald Bogle in *Toms, Coons, Mulattoes, Mammies and Bucks* wrote:

> It is now evident that *The Green Pastures* rested on a cruel assumption: that nothing could be more ludicrous than transporting the lowly language and folkways of the early twentieth-century Negro back to the high stately world before the flood... And in this juxtaposition of low with high, there were implied Negro ignorance and inferiority.

However, the sheer dynamics of the cast drew firm admiration.

Lynn Riggs

Possibly the only play – described as a 'folk comedy' – for which Riggs is remembered is *Green Grow the Lilacs* (1931). Lynn Riggs was a mixed-blood Cherokee living in Indian Territory in Oklahoma, a cattle rancher's son, who later dramatised the life he knew from his early experience. His intention was to 'recapture in a kind of nostalgic glow...the great range of mood which characterized the old folk songs and ballads'. In 1943 Oscar Hammerstein II worked for the first time with Richard Rodgers, adapting the script as a musical and retitling it *Oklahoma!* 'I kept many of the lines of the original play,' he wrote in the *New York Times* (4 September 1943), 'without making any changes in them at all for the simple reason that they could not be improved on – at any rate, not by me. Lynn Riggs and *Green Grow the Lilacs* are the very soul of *Oklahoma!*'. The play text was presented as a movie in 1955.

Lillian Hellman

Lillian Hellman has been described as 'a smoker, a drinker, a lover and a fighter'; she was also one of America's most challenging playwrights. She briefly attended Columbia and New York University before working in a publishing house. Her first play, *The Children's Hour* (1934) was written with the help of her companion Dashiell Hammett, telling of two teachers in a boarding school who are accused by a student of having a lesbian relationship. Totally shamed by this revelation, one of the teachers kills herself. Not primarily a play about sexuality, it examines the abuse of power and the effect of this on sufferers. Over seven hundred performances were given on Broadway and seventy years later touring productions are often to be found. Her second big success, *The Little Foxes* (1939), was also concerned with control, this time of a family business by three siblings. Here was an indictment of a subject to which Hellman often referred, capitalist motives and the rise to power of the middle class, seen in terms of blackmail, sexual manipulation and murder, but beyond this melodrama the writer also studied the inner lives and struggles of her characters. They were rumoured at the time of production to relate to Hellman's own Southern family.

During the second world war *Watch on the Rhine* (1941) dealt with the rise of the fascists and America's tardiness in taking up arms against Hitler and Mussolini. A strong leftist, Hellman – on suspicion of supporting Communism – was subpoenaed to appear in the 1950s before Senator McCarthy's committee dealing with un-American activities. The latter years of her life were spent in writing several non-fiction books, partly autobiographical in which *Pentimento* (1973), an account of some of her friends, and *Scoundrel Times*, about McCarthyism, figured.

Clifford Odets

At fifteen Odets became a member of the left-wing New York Theatre Guild and in 1931 a founder member of the Group Theatre where method-actor Lee Strasberg was a guru. The aim of the Group Theatre was to establish a permanent company, encouraging new writers and new plays which would express some of the social and political ideas of its members. Strasberg introduced many of the theatre concepts of Konstantin Stanislavsky, his former mentor. Odets rapidly found success and fame here with his one-act play *Waiting for Lefty* (1935), performed at Manhattan's Civic Repertory Theatre. The short play focuses on a pre-strike union meeting of the city's taxi drivers; while they wait for the popular Lefty Costello to arrive to address them, the capitalist agent Harry Fatt attempts to thwart the planned dissent. Half-a-dozen episodic scenes, each ending with a blackout, sketch the causes of the discontent, hanging mainly on corrupt practice and injustice. Before the piece ended the production prompted the unrehearsed audience, too, to call for strike action. Brief it may have been but the piece served as a mirror of the times: America was sinking under the Great Depression with workers existing on meagre wages, a point brought to the fore in John Steinbeck's novel *The Grapes of Wrath* (1939). From 1934 Odets was a member of the American Communist Party and there are echoes of Karl Marx and Friedrich Engels in the dialogue of *Waiting for Lefty. Till the Day I Die* (1935) was written to be played in the same bill as *Waiting for Lefty*, sharing with it qualities of agit-prop theatre (theatre which attempts to change the ideological viewpoint of the audience by using propaganda and agitation). It celebrates the communist resistance to the German nazi party. After the second world war, as Hellman had been, he was summoned to appear before the Un-American Activities Committee; unlike her he was 'co-operative'. As he aged, more writing of film scripts and scenarios caused a diminution of his output of plays. However, those he wrote took on more of a 'realist' tinge than the couple of early works which so assuredly established his reputation.

Tennessee Williams

The characters in Tennessee Williams' plays are bound up with the life of their author. He was born in 1911 at Columbus, Mississippi in the American South, the child of a puritanical mother, and his grandfather was an Episcopalian rector. In his early life Williams was surrounded by women, including his sister Rose – she was the model for characters in several of his plays – and elderly people. The family moved to St Louis when Williams was fourteen and the occasion was marked by the gift of a typewriter from his mother. Writing he saw as an 'escape from the world of reality in which [he] felt acutely uncomfortable'. As a young teenager Williams became an avid film supporter, later weaving cinematic techniques into his stage directions: sound, light and colour became symbols, used to evoke moods. After some short-term jobs Williams graduated from the Universities of Washington and Iowa at the age of twenty-seven. 1944 brought success in the form of *The Glass Menagerie* performed in Chicago and then on Broadway.

The play's action centres on Tom (a parallel of Williams), his unbendingly moral mother Amanda and Laura (the parallel of Rose), a diffident and at times hysterical girl who collects fragile glass miniatures of animals. Before he abandons his sister Tom is given the task of setting Laura up with a fiancé but his ability to find someone suitable, after an abject mistake, fails him. Tom's evenings are spent at the cinema and his physical means of gaining freedom from the apartment is the fire escape. At the end of the play there is one last descent by this method; the steps illustrate the divide between the outside world and Amanda's enclosure.

A Streetcar Named Desire (1947) followed next, winning the Pulitzer Prize, the money from which bought Williams a home in Key West, an escape route to a quiet haven for writing and relaxation. The narrative tells of the gradual disintegration of Blanche DuBois, an isolate, as was Williams, seeking oblivion to some degree in liquor and self-delusion but instead having forced upon her anger, lust and rape. Eventually committed to a mental hospital, she remarks to the doctor at curtain-fall: 'Whoever you are – I have always depended on the kindness of strangers.' There is a similar line that Williams came across in a play he read: 'We're all of us sentenced to solitary confinement in our own skins,' and as he repeated it, he chuckled. *Cat on a Hot Tin Roof* (1955) differs from the former as it is a study of family relationships, claustrophobic, complicated and crowded; set in the Mississippi Delta, it is a story of wealth and the problems of inheritance and primogeniture. Big Daddy is near to death. His daughter-in-law, Maggie, the 'cat' of the title, is ruthlessly greedy, both rapacious and lusting. This was a play laid open for critics to attack its 'excesses', a way of making veiled criticisms of his gayness of which Williams made no secret and for a decade he lived with Frank Merlo, his lover, until the younger man's death from lung cancer in 1961.

The violence of some of his plays caused comment, too, but Williams viewed this as part of the human condition; on the other hand he acknowledged that the plots would only work in their particular American settings. Different levels of aggression are expressed in *Suddenly Last Summer* (1958): there is the subterranean violence of the family that Catharine Holley has married into; the surgical violence of the lobotomy she has suffered; the violence of the interaction between Sebastian and the beach children at Cabeza de Lobo who eventually murder him and – in the tradition of a number of Greek tragedies – cannibalise his body. As if this leaves the audience unsated, there is the symbolic violence of the jungle plants in Mrs Venables's conservatory:

> There are massive tree-flowers that suggest organs of a body, torn out, still glistening with undried blood; there are harsh cries and sibilant hissings and thrashing sounds in the garden as if it were inhabited by beasts, serpents and birds, all of savage nature...

Williams worked himself almost to death and alongside this he was a heavy drug user. His ending was an accident: he choked on the lid of a bottle of pills he was taking. Much of his life was lived in and around St Louis in the deep south and it has become a matter of pride to residents that a writer who has gradually achieved acclaim should have won this in their shared neighbourhood.

Arthur Miller

Harlem was Miller's birthplace, in the second decade of the twentieth century, then an elegant district of New York with open spaces and a mix of races. He graduated at Michigan where he began his craft of playwriting and later transferred his place of residence to the Connecticut hills. Generally he is labelled a 'social dramatist' and his dislike of the effects of the capitalist system rebounding on the poor of the cities encourages the further label of 'Marxist'. His wide output of plays encourages one to be highly selective in a choice of a few – from a possible range of novels, short stories, dramas, reportage, one-act plays and essays – on which comment can be offered.

One of the earliest of his plays which gained lasting approbation following a long run on Broadway and a translation to film, double-starring Edward G Robinson and Burt Lancaster, was *All My Sons* (1947) in which the audience was presented with a moral issue and an inevitable and suitable punishment: Joe Keller, a manufacturer of defective aeroplane parts during the second world war causes the death of twenty-seven aviators. Keller is legally exonerated and attempts to live within the community as though the catastrophe had not happened, only to have his son, Chris, question him about the sordid business. Having fought in the war Chris has a different vision to his father of the social responsibility of the individual. However, the play is 'about' more than this narrative line: Christopher Bigsby summarises the subtext:

>...this is also a play about betrayal...about America, about self-deceit, about self righteousness, about egotism presented as idealism, about a fear of mortality, about guilt...[1]

In an introduction to the play Miller has pointed out that Keller is not simply amoral but that he is an isolate within society, living within 'the fortress of unrelatedness'.[2]

There are affinities between *All my Sons* and Miller's next play *Death of a Salesman* (1949) although the latter is not an attack on capitalism but a study of a man, Willy Loman, disillusioned by the results of the passage of time and the way in which this has robbed him of his dreams. A word should be said at this juncture about the 'great American dream': in the early years of the twentieth century America seemed to hold open its doors to the dispossessed of the world, offering them the opportunity to earn a decent wage, enjoy a comfortable lifestyle and engage in that freedom which would allow each man to shape his own destiny. Loman's father had been the hopeful immigrant and his son was the unfulfilled hero who never lost the thread of aspiration passed from one generation to the next. He may be seen as an example of the 'tragic hero', a notion stemming back to classical Greek plays, in which the hero, a man of noble birth, displays that he has a flaw in his character that eventually is his undoing. Whatever the externals of location and event, the kernel of the tragedy is the fall of the hero to whom Miller often gives a title, here the Salesman. Although Loman cannot boast a noble birth – Miller said of this that it 'matters not at all whether a modern play concerns itself with a grocer or a president, whether the hero falls from a great height or a small one' – he has his aspirations, so making an audience ask, 'What do men live for?' In presenting the story Miller adopts a filmic technique, setting the play within the Lomans' house and yard, yet using this area to explore the past as well as the present. In his description of the scene Miller almost writes as though his first stage directions were the introduction to a novel:

We are aware of towering angular shapes behind [Loman's house], *surrounding it on all sides. Only the blue light of the sky falls upon the house and forestage; the surrounding area shows an angry glow of orange. As more light appears we see a solid vault of apartment houses around the small, fragile-seeming home. An air of dream clings to the place, a dream rising out of reality.*

In the narration of the plot symbolism often shines out from the realism of the situation as the audience learns of Loman's tragic life, not told in poetic phrases but in harsh, uncultured terms that make their own impact. Writing fifty years after the opening of *Death of a Salesman*, Miller told of the difficulty he feared members of the audience might have in discerning whether Loman was imagining or living through one or other of the play's scenes. He found the same problem when he prepared a production for the stage of the Beijing People's Art Theatre: but although the muddle can occur in reading the play, its real dramatic nature was only appreciated when seen in performance.[3]

One of Miller's most frequently staged plays is *The Crucible* (1953), although its initial Broadway run was for 197 performances only. The drama spoke of the Salem women tried for witchcraft in late seventeenth-century New England and of Proctor, the flawed hero of the play. This event in the past acted as a parable for the America of the mid-twentieth century in which Senator McCarthy presided over the House Un-American Activities Committee which considered reputed dealings of well-known citizens, especially those connected with the arts, with Communism. Miller claimed that if he had not written the play the enquiry would be unregistered in American literature at any popular level: he had, he said, 'made something lasting out of a violent but brief turmoil'.[4]

Two further plays should be briefly mentioned. *A View from the Bridge* (1955) tells of the illegal entry into the United States of two longshoremen continuing the theme he often uses of man against society and the ultimate sighting of the premise that man equals society. Like Sophocles and later Shakespeare he tries to 'draw a whole world into one man, to bring a national experience to bear on an individual subject'.[5] *The Misfits* (1961) is better known as a novel and as a film. Written originally as a film script for Miller's wife Marilyn Monroe – an unhappy marriage that was eventually to be dissolved – it appropriately deals with a beautiful woman in Nevada who, whilst suing for a divorce, falls in love with three hired hands who herd old horses and take them to the knacker's yard. The play examines her relationships with the three men and her feelings for the animals. In addition to Monroe, two other notable film stars appeared, Clark Gable and Montgomery Clift. In spite of its filmic origin *The Misfits* required voice-over narration which frequently over-stated the point:

> [Isabelle's] nose and cheeks are faintly purpled, her voice cracks and pipes, and she looks on the world with an amused untidiness that approaches an air of wreckage and misspent intelligence.[6]

In spite of having as director so eminent a practitioner as John Huston, the structure seemed loose and the film appeared without form and direction. But to keep criticism in perspective one must hold in mind Miller's aphorism: 'I have often rescued a sense of reality by recalling Chekhov's remark: "If I had listened to the critics I'd have died drunk in the gutter".'[7]

T S Eliot

It can be easy for English people to forget that T S Eliot was, by birth in St Louis, an American and that he gained his first degree at Harvard University, following this by study at the Sorbonne in Paris, and Merton College, Oxford. In 1927 he became a British subject. The survey in the previous chapter contains some notes on T S Eliot and students working on American twentieth-century literature are recommended to study these as well as the bibliography lists.

Edward Albee

Edward Albee was adopted by Reed Albee, a vaudeville theatre owner who also happened to be a millionaire. His education was expensive but he profited little from it and it was left to Thornton Wilder to encourage him to undertake serious writing for the theatre. This he did, much under the influence of European writers of the theatre of the absurd movement. In 1959 his short play, *The Zoo Story*, was presented in Berlin and then in New York, an accurate study of a layabout guy with schizophrenia, an image of a solitary man's loneliness and inability to make contact with an executive class representative whose presence on a bench in Central Park he disturbs. A wider range of writing followed including full-length plays. Sufficient here that two are briefly noted: *Who's Afraid of Virginia Woolf?* (1962) and *Tiny Alice* (1964).

Virginia Woolf employs two married couples, a pattern of relationship of which Albee is fond although in this instance much of what we might expect to find in the interaction is present but somewhat wildly decorated. George and Martha have academic backgrounds; they entertain a younger couple, Nick and Honey, again university teachers, to a night of fraught drinking. Each act of the play suggests the advancing progress of the relationships from 'Fun and Games', through

'Walpurgisnacht' to 'The Exorcism'. The childless older couple have created a fantasy son (21 years old) to off-set their deprivation and their plight is mirrored in Honey's phantom pregnancy. Although there is an obvious advancement, the strange keeping-in-balance of the two pairs reminds the audience of a similar tidiness in the writing of Eugène Ionesco; Martin Esslin, the historian of absurdist drama has compared Albee's views of the marital battle with those of August Strindberg and Eugene O'Neill.

Tiny Alice is an altogether more complicated plot and puzzled many who saw the play as well as John Gielgud who first took the role of Brother Julian. The plot concerns Miss Alice, the world's richest woman, who makes a deal to donate to the church one billion dollars a year. In some of the scenes in a replica of an English castle one sees a miniature version of the building within which future events are at times enacted. This conceit is clear but one of the difficulties for the audience was to work out the moral stance of the various characters.

Timberlake Wertenbaker

To conclude, here is one suggestion of a play by Timberlake Wertenbaker, who was born of Anglo-American parents. A single play gives one an impression of the various characteristics of this author: she is obviously interested in the struggles of women in a world dominated by men; historical characters hold a fascination for her whether factual or fictional and the way in which the story is told matters as much as the material content of it. *Our Country's Good* (1988) is the story of an Australian penal settlement and the attempt of the transportees to stage a production of George Farquhar's play *The Recruiting Officer* (1706). The fascinating cross-referencing between the inner play and its actors holds a Brechtian effect. How much this reflects an actual performance given by convicts in 1804 and seen by Robert Eastwick, the master of the trading vessel Betsy, is difficult to judge. In his journal Eastwick noted:

> The colonists…had a theatre, and under the patronage of Governor King, gave several representations during the time I was there, all very tolerably acted. Amongst other plays I remember witnessing Farquhar's comedy of *The Recruiting Officer* and the entertainment of *The Virgin Unmasked*, both affording very excellent amusement.[8]

Some American novelists

In order that the reflection of events in the time of the novelist may be appreciated the following writers and a sample of their work are presented in approximate date order. Of course, this is less needful when looking at period novels, although many writers contrast current ideas with their historic counterparts.

Theodore Dreiser was born into a family that embodied poverty and respectability; as he grew up he yearned for social acceptance and wealth. He worked as a newspaper reporter in Chicago, New York and Pittsburgh, studying the novels of Honoré de Balzac when time allowed. His first novel, *Sister Carrie* (1900), the life of an actress who marries a man descending the social scale as appositely she rises, shocked Dreiser's publisher (Doubleday) who withheld it from circulation because of the heroine's amoral stance. Several of his other early novels centre on the difficulties, if not impossibility, of youthful success; his extended family provided many of the portraits used in these early works.

It was the aim of Henry James' father to make his sons 'citizens of the world' and the widely separated townscapes of the settings of James' novels points to the success of his objective. *The Wings of the Dove* (1902) is located in London and Venice where one sees the situation – almost operatic – of the dying Milly Theale kept alive by hope and the love of Martin Densher, an impoverished journalist. A strong line of irony runs through the book and on its style Andrew Taylor has remarked:

> [The] prose is characterized by the increased length and complexity of sentences; multiple clauses serve to incessantly pursue and refine meaning, such that facts remain tentative, intention fluid, and conclusions evanescent.[9]

The novel eventually became the basis for an opera in 1961 by Douglas Moore. The scope of James' work was wide, beginning with reviews of fiction and theatre, plays, short stories and critical studies. Somewhat surprisingly in 1899 James left London, where he had decided to live, for Lamb House, an elegant Georgian building in Rye, Sussex. Leon Edel has written a five-volume biography (1953–72) of James.

Edith Wharton was a member of a distinguished New York family, privately educated and influenced by Henry James. Her book *The House of Mirth* (1905) tells of a girl in Wharton's home city intent on achieving a brilliant marriage. Conventional standards are broken and in consequence society ostracises Lily Bart. As with much of James' work, Wharton has produced a study in the acceptance of false values.

A wild life, sailing his sloop around San Francisco Bay to raid oyster beds, was the background to the early days of Jack London, related in his two autobiographical works *The Cruise of the Dazzler* (1902) and *Tales of the Fish Patrol* (1905). Reminiscent of Kipling, one of London's most popular novels, *The Call of the Wild* (1903), tells of Buck, a dog in the far north who escapes from civilisation eventually to lead a wolf pack. He is the canine equivalent to the Nietzshean supermen who fascinated London.

On his own admission Jesus, Hamlet and Shelley shaped the thought and aspirations of Upton Sinclair. The lack of moral stances which weakened American city society was one of the targets for this writer whose early novel, *The Jungle* (1906) exposed corruption in the Chicago meat-packing industry. The vivid descriptions of the interior of the works surround the reader with the clanger of machines and livestock and the book made such an impact that legislation for reform was put into operation.

The missionary enterprises of the Roman Catholic Church in New Mexico were researched by Willa Cather and furnished material for her book *Death Comes for the Archbishop* (1927). Careful in its presentation of period, the book tells of the foundation of the diocese of New Mexico. The triumph of the bishop and the vicar-general over the apathy of the native Indians and the opposition of corrupt Spanish priests helps to create a gripping tension. Never a Catholic herself, Cather seems to have enjoyed a natural affinity with the spirituality of the Spanish missioners in America.

A further period novel published posthumously at much the same time as the former is *Billy Budd* (1924) by Herman Melville. Budd is the handsome and heroic sailor lad of the eighteenth-century ballad haunted by evil, in the guise of Petty Officer Claggart, to Budd's consternation. Billy eventually delivers his infamous and fatal blow to Claggart and suffers the inevitable punishment.

To write of an ageing woman's rejuvenation by means of a glandular operation shocked American readers in the 1920s. Gertrude Atherton's *Black Oxen* (1923), a society novel, offered but one subject amongst the many genres she pursued such as the Spanish settlements in California, romantic short stories, biographies – some fictional – essays and historical works. *Atherton* (1979) by Charlotte S McClure offers a critical study.

Possibly the boy Hemingway, with his fishing and hunting expeditions from school, was attempting to recreate himself; spells of journalism and work in an ambulance unit in France helped to colour the inner landscapes of his later stories. The moral collapse of a group of American and English expatriates is explored in *The Sun Also Rises* (1926), sometimes titled in the United Kingdom *Fiesta* (1927). Representatives of this 'lost generation', a phrase used by Gertrude Stein, are examined in biographical detail as they attempt to make their way to Pamplona for the bullfights. Brett's romance with a young matador, Pedro Romero, is one of the romantic interests of the plot but it ends prematurely when she returns to Michael Campbell, 'one of her own kind'.

Another 'journeying account', *As I Lay Dying* (1930) by William Faulkner, is set amongst an impoverished white family on a pilgrimage to bury their mother in her native Jefferson. The individual adventures and excitements of the children undertaking this are traced until the reader reaches the highlight, the attempt of Darl to cremate his mother's body by setting fire to a barn where Addie's coffin rests. A strong sense of unease runs through the narrative that intensifies with the capture of Darl and his incarceration in an asylum. The novels Faulkner produced in the 1930s serve as key works to substantiate the claim that here is the greatest American novelist of the twentieth century but at the time their reception was subdued and Faulkner moved to Hollywood where he worked with the film director Howard Hawks.

The characters in William Saroyan's novels enjoy a sentimental exaltation, representing something of the writer himself who like many of the roles was an Armenian-American working-class fellow. An early example of his work is *The Daring Young Man on the Flying Trapeze*

(1934). Critics often point to the rhapsodic quality of Saroyan's writing and his strong ability to create a mood.

A couple of novels written prior to the second world war, *Tortilla Flat* (1935) and *The Grapes of Wrath* (1939) give an indication of the writing of John Steinbeck. The first is set in the world of the *paisanos*, a native people combining Spanish, Indian and Mexican bloods found in the hills of Monterey where they live a wild amoral life, often drunk and sexually promiscuous. Friendship is supreme, countered by a love for the Church. The second novel is also located in California, the land of plenty, and speaks of a refugee family from the dust bowl of Oklahoma, struggling against exploitation as its members attempt to find work. This picaresque novel, conceived on a vast scale, proclaims the invincibility of the human spirit in the form of Ma Joad who triumphantly asserts near the end: 'We ain't gonna die out. People is goin' on – changin' a little, maybe, but going right on.'

A quartet of originals pass through *The Heart is a Lonely Hunter* (1940), the first novel of Carson McCullers. A deaf-mute, John Singer, in a small Georgia town loses his only friend when committed to an asylum; Biff, an impotent man, Jake, a Communist and an alcoholic wanderer, Mick, an adolescent and Dr Benedict Copeland, an intellectual black man each makes his way to Singer, looking for understanding and finding some kind of recognition. Evident compassion and individualism with the story instantly appealed to readers, the more so as it reflected the alarming strokes McCullers suffered in her twenties. The writer described her novel, the first she had written, as an 'ironic parable of fascism'.

Truman Capote needs little by way of introduction. *Other Voices, Other Rooms* (1948), an early work, highlights the quest of a gay lad to find his real nature at his home on a Louisiana plantation. Reality and fantasy help him to come to terms with himself. Travel and biography figure strongly in Capote's body of work, including several accounts, factual, of murders.

A first work which caught the attention of its time and a young readership was *The Catcher in the Rye* (1951) by J D Salinger, again a story of teenage unhappiness and uncertainty which can only be resolved by an escape, this time from boarding school. Holden Caulfield's encounters with past pupils and friends, as well as with a former English teacher, form the body of the tale.

Another immature young man, Harry Angstrom, former high school basket ball champion and now a kitchen appliance demonstrator, is to be found in the cycle by John Updike which began with *Rabbit, Run* (1960). The life of the Angstroms, Harry, known as Rabbit, and his alcoholic wife, are demonstrated at ten year intervals in *Rabbit, Redux* (1971), *Run Rabbit Run* (1981) and finally *Rabbit at Rest* (1990). By the third volume society has accepted Angstrom by conferring a country club membership. Incident and irony, one upholding the other, are rich in the books.

Although Saul Bellow was educated at the University of Chicago he was born in Canada, the child of Russian émigrés. How much of *Herzog* (1964) is factual autobiography is open to question: a middle-aged Jewish intellectual reveals his relationships, mostly through letters and journals with two former wives and other women, with his children and a friend as well as speaking intimately of Herzog's careers as a writer and history teacher. From a Jewish milieu Herzog has to adapt to a Western Christian background that reinforces his belief that 'there are displaced persons everywhere'. The narrative line is a curious mix of seriousness and comic situation. A further autobiographical cipher Bellow creates is the protagonist of *The Dean's December* (1983).

A great traveller, Paul Theroux ploughs his adventures into his writing, either in legitimate travel works – *The Great Railway Bazaar* (1975) describing a journey through Europe and Russia to Japan is an example – or in novels. The central character of *The Mosquito Coast* (1982), a contender for Theroux's 'best novel', is an American engineer seeking a new life in the jungles of Honduras.

Ancient Evenings (1983) marked Norman Mailer's return to the novel after twenty years of writing about the American character. The reader of this 'historical' epic is taken to the ancient Egypt of three thousand years ago.

A selection of twentieth-century American poets

Although Robert Frost was born in San Francisco in 1874, his parents relocated to New Hampshire when he was ten and the young Frost had the chance to try many craft-based occupations from an early age. Craftsmanship interested him whether it centred on making shoes or, alongside this rural life, writing poems. These, he hoped, had an air of no nonsense realism about them: 'There are two types of realist – the one who offers a good deal of dirt with his potato to show that it is a real one; and the one who is satisfied with the potato brushed clean.' For Frost art did the latter; it cleaned his poetry potato and stripped it to form. His poems have a directness that seems to eliminate complexity but they do pose questions as in the apparently simple piece 'Stopping by Woods on a Snowy Evening':

Whose woods these are I think I know,
His house is in the village though;
He will not see me stopping here
To watch his woods fill up with snow.

My little horse must think it queer
To stop without a farmhouse near

Between the woods and frozen lake
The darkest evening of the year.

It continues for two more verses but already the reader is left wondering about the mysterious owner of the woods and the equally mystifying rider who, it transpires, has many miles to ride before he can lay down to sleep.

Bohemian behaviour saw the end of Ezra Pound's career at Wabash College where he lectured in Spanish and French. He had been born in Idaho in 1885 and after his teaching interlude he removed to Italy in 1908. That same year he took up residence in London for twelve years and then lived until the end of World War II in Rapallo, Italy. The broadcasts he made from here were considered treasonable so the Americans, when they took Italy, caged Pound and then removed him to America where he was declared insane and detained outside Washington at St Elizabeth's Hospital. Place did not have a strong influence on his work but the ideas of those who lived there or those who visited him formed the body of his thought and writing. Much of the latter was in prose, fired by a variety of enthusiasms: Provençal troubadour ballads, Japanese drama, the sculptor Gaudier-Brzeska, economics, Jefferson's financial theories, as well as numerous translations. T S Eliot and Pound influenced each other, garnering their experiences and experimenting with writing. Allusion became an important element of style and in *Canto 1* alliteration (a repetition of the same consonant) is used reminding one of Anglo-Saxon battle poetry:

Dark blood flowed in the fosse,
Souls out of Erebus, cadaverous dead, of brides
Of youths and of the old who had borne much;
Souls stained with recent tears, girls tender,
Men many...

Rightly, critics declared the cantos to be the apotheosis of Pound's life's work.

Laura Riding is a disappointed but interesting phenomenon. Born in New York City in 1901 she attended Cornell University and for a short period was married to Louis Gottschalk, a history tutor there. After their divorce she went to live on Mallorca where she edited several works in conjunction with Robert Graves; then there was a return to Florida. Her early verse was collected into a number of volumes until she decided that poetry was not, for her, the vehicle of truth on which she had pinned her hopes. Thirty years of silence followed after which she partly came to terms with the difficulties she had encountered, although as the following lines show, all was not resolved:

> With the face goes a mirror
> As with the mind a world.
> Likeness tells the doubting eye
> That strangeness is not strange,
> At an early hour and knowledge
> Identity not yet familiar
> Looks back upon itself from later,
> And seems itself.

Maya Angelou was born in St Louis in 1928 and established herself as a performer, singer, dancer and playwright, as well as a writer of plays and poems. She has a special skill in presenting her own personality, that of a young black woman in America as well as in Egypt and Ghana where she also lived.

A rebellion by poets against conventional society was to be found in the Beat Generation – a term coined by the novelist Jack Kerouac – with their centres in New York and San Francisco. This anti-authoritarian disaffection was fired by drink and drugs and writers evolved their own vocabulary, street phrases combined with terms from Buddhism, by then an established cult for drop-outs. One of the leading lights of the movement was Allen Ginsberg who became its spokesman in the 1960s. His working area included the urban poor and the Jewish milieu. On the death of his mother, a Russian émigrée who suffered from bouts of madness, he wrote a Kaddish or Hebrew intercession for the dead to honour her into which he poured much of his acquired philosophy:

> ...And how Death is that remedy all singers dream
> of, sing, remember, prophesy as in the Hebrew Anthem,
> or the Buddhist Book of Answers – and my own
> imagination of a withered leaf – at dawn – ...

Columbia helped to form Ginsberg but he also travelled to India where he could study Zen Buddhism; he saw as important his other wanderings which gave him the opportunity to work as a dish-washer, night porter, welder, seaman and book reviewer for *Newsweek*. A great exuberance fired him and he took up various causes such as gay rights, civil rights and the peace movement. His *Collected Poems* were published in 1985.

Although their work is totally dissimilar, autobiography links Sylvia Plath with Ted Hughes. Plath gained a scholarship which admitted her to Smith College. Whilst there she suffered a nervous breakdown but nevertheless, after an intermission, managed to finish her course. A further exhibition took her to England where she studied at Newnham College, Cambridge, married Ted Hughes, had two children and then unexpectedly took her own life. In her poems she abandons middle class diction, instead taking refuge in images that become part of her confessional make-up. She peers at the fog-bound countryside of 'Sheep in Fog' and instantly adapts the picture to her own personal feelings:

The hills step off into whiteness.
People or stars
Regard me sadly, I disappoint them...
My bones hold a stillness, the far
Fields melt my heart.
They threaten
To let me through to a heaven
Starless and fatherless, a dark water.

This dark water of death is often considered. She even refers to herself as Mrs Lazarus (Lazarus was the young man whose tomb Jesus entered in order to raise him from the dead) and a reader is soon convinced Plath had the strongest of premonitions about the nature of her own death.

2.   SELECTED AMERICAN AUTHORS, PLAYWRIGHTS AND WORKS OF THE TWENTIETH CENTURY

Note: Titles of plays and musicals are preceded by an asterisk.

1900:   Sister Carrie by Theodore Dreiser

    1901:   First transatlantic radio

1902:   The Wings of the Dove by Henry James

1902:   The Cruise of the Dazzler by Jack London

1903:   The Call of the Wild by Jack London

    1904:   American Academy of Arts and Letters

1905:   Tales of the Fish Patrol by Jack London

1905:   The House of Mirth by Edith Wharton

    1906:   Earthquake in San Francisco

1906:   The Jungle by Upton Sinclair

    1907:   First Ziegfeld Follies

    1909:   Model T Ford marks first mass production of automobiles

1914: Panama Canal opened

1915: Provincetown and Washington Square Players founded

1915: Spoon River Anthology by Edgar Lee Masters

1916: First issue of Theatre Arts Magazine

1917: America enters World War 1

1918: Theatre Guild established

1918: Armistice

1919: 18th amendment: prohibition of liquor

1920: 19th amendment: votes for women

1920: *The Emperor Jones by Eugene O'Neill

1922: Coal and railway strikes

1922: The Waste Land by T S Eliot

1923: Black Oxen by Gertrude Atherton

1923: New Hampshire by Robert Frost

1923: History of American Drama by Quinn

1924: Billy Budd by Herman Melville

1924: *Desire under the Elms by Eugene O'Neill

1924: *Beggar on Horseback by S Kaufman and Marc Connelly

1925: An American Tragedy by Theodore Dreiser, dramatised the following year by Patrick Kearney

1926: The Sun Also Rises by Ernest Hemingway

1926: *The Great God Brown by Eugene O'Neill

1926: Book of the Month Club founded

1928: First Mickey Mouse cartoon

1929: Wall Street Crash

1927: Death Comes for the Archbishop by Willa Cather

1929: A Farewell to Arms by Ernest Hemingway

1930: *Green Pastures by Marc Connelly

1930: As I Lay Dying by William Faulkner

1931:   *Green Grow the Lilacs by Lynn Riggs

1932:   Tobacco Road by Erskine Calwell, dramatised the following year by Jack Kirkland

1933:   *Alien Corn by Sidney Howard

1934:   *The Children's Hour by Lillian Hellman

1934:   *The Petrified Forest by Robert Sherwood

1934:   The Daring Young Man on the Flying Trapeze by William Saroyan

    1935:   Regular trans-Pacific air service established

1935:   Tortilla Flat by John Steinbeck, dramatised in 1937 by Jack Kirkland

1935:   *Winterset by Maxwell Anderson

1935:   *Waiting for Lefty by Clifford Odets

1936:   *Bury the Dead by Irwin Shaw

1938:   *Our Town by Thornton Wilder

1938:   Collected Poems by Laura Riding

    1939:   King George VI and Queen Elizabeth tour US and Canada

1939:   The Grapes of Wrath by John Steinbeck

1939:   Collected Poems by Robert Frost

    1940:   Limited national emergency declared; refugee children from Europe admitted to US as 'visitors'

1940:   The Heart is a Lonely Hunter by Carson McCullers

    1941:   Japanese attack on Pearl Harbour

1941:   *Watch on the Rhine by Lillian Hellman

1942:   *This is the Army by Isaiah Berlin

    1943:   Italian armistice

1943:   *Oklahoma! by Richard Rodgers and Oscar Hammerstein II

1945:   *The Glass Menagerie by Tennessee Williams

    1945:   United Nations charter written

1947:   *A Streetcar Named Desire by Tennessee Williams

1948:   Other Voices, Other Rooms by Truman Capote

1949:   *Death of a Salesman by Arthur Miller

      1950:   Peace treaty with Japan

1950:   *The Cocktail Party by T S Eliot

1951:   The Catcher in the Rye by J D Salinger

1951:   The Ballad of the Sad Café by Carson McCullers, dramatised in 1963 by Edward Albee

      1952:   Investigations in US into un-American activities

1955:   *Bus Stop by William Inge

1955:   *A View from the Bridge by Arthur Miller

1955:   *Cat on a Hot Tin Roof by Tennessee Williams

1956:   *Long Day's Journey into Night by Eugene O'Neill

1958:   *Suddenly Last Summer by Tennessee Williams

1960:   Rabbit, Run by John Updike

1962:   *The Night of the Iguana by Tennessee Williams

1962:   *Who's Afraid of Virginia Woolf? by Edward Albee

      1963:   President John F Kennedy assassinated

1964:   Herzog by Saul Bellow

1965:   *Tiny Alice by Edward Albee

      1968:   Protests against American military involvement in Vietnam

1970:   Collected Cantos by Ezra Pound

      1973:   Vietnam War ends

1975:   The Great Railway Bazaar by Paul Theroux

1975:   Letters Home by Sylvia Plath

1977:   Johnny Panic and the Bible of Dreams by Sylvia Plath

1981:   Collected Poems by Sylvia Plath

1982:   The Mosquito Coast by Paul Theroux

1983:   Ancient Evenings by Norman Mailer

1983:   Why Don't You Sing? by Maya Angelou

1984:   Collected Poems, 1947–1980 by Allen Ginsberg

3.   BIBLIOGRAPHY

General works

Atkinson, Brooks, *Broadway Scrapbook*. New York: Theatre Arts, 1947.

Bogle, Donald, *Toms, Coons, Mulattoes, Mammies and Bucks*. Oxford: Roundhouse, 1994.

Bordman, Gerald, *The Concise Oxford Companion to American Theatre*. New York: Oxford University Press, 1987.

Cohn, Ruby, *New American Dramatists, 1960–80*. New York: Grove, 1982.

Downer, Alan S, *Fifty Years of American Drama, 1900–1950*. Chicago: Henry Regnery, 1951.

Garfield, David, *A Player's Place, the Story of the Actors' Studio*. New York: Macmillan, 1980.

Gassner, John, *Form and Ideas in Modern Theatre*. New York: Holt, Reinhart and Winston [1965].

Harris, Andrew B, *Broadway Theatre*. London and New York: Routledge, 1994.

McCarthy, Mary, *Sights and Spectacles, 1937–56*. New York: Farrar, Straus and Cudahy, 1956.

Savran, David, *In their Own Words: Contemporary American Playwrights*. New York: TGC, 1988.

Smith, Wendy, *Real Life Drama: The Group Theatre and America, 1931–40*. New York: Alfred A Knopf, 1990.

Stagg, Jerry, *The Brothers Schubert*. New York: Random House, 1968.

Taubman, Howard, *The Making of the American Theatre*. New York: Howard McCann, 1965.

Weales, Gerald, *The Jumping Off Place: American Drama in the 1960s*. New York: Macmillan, 1969.

Weaver, Jace, *That the People Might Live: Native American Literature*. Oxford: Oxford University Press, 1997.

Playwrights: biography and criticism

Albee, Edward

Roudané, Matthew C, *Understanding Edward Albee*. Columbia, SC: University of South Carolina, 1987.

Hecht, Ben

Hecht, Ben, *A Child of the Century*. New York: Simon and Schuster, 1954.

Hellman, Lillian

Armato, Philip M, 'Good and Evil in Lillian Hellman's *The Children's Hour*,' *Education Theatre Journal*, 25 (1973), 443–7.

Estrin, Mark W, ed, *Critical Essays on Lillian Hellman*. Boston: G K Hall, 1989.

Hellman, Lillian, *An Unfinished Woman: A Memoir*. London: Quartet Books, 1977.

Riordan, Mary M, *Lillian Hellman: A Bibliography*. New Jersey: Scarecrow Press, 1980.

Lederer, Katherine, *Lillian Hellman*. Boston: Twayne, 1979.

Miller, Arthur

Bigsby, Christopher, ed, *The Cambridge Companion to Arthur Miller*. Cambridge: Cambridge University Press, 1997.

Corrigan, Robert, *Arthur Miller: A Collection of Critical Essays*. Englewood Cliffs: Prentice Hall, 1969.

Goode, James, *The Story of the Misfits*. Indianapolis: Bobbs-Merrill, 1963.

Hunt, Albert, 'Realism and Intelligence: some notes on Arthur Miller', in *Encore*, London: 7 (1960), pp 12 ff.

Miller, Arthur, *The Theatre Essays of Arthur Miller*. New York: Penguin Books, 1978.

Murray, Edward, *The Cinematic Imagination*. New York: Frederick Ungar, 1972.

Welland, Dennis, *Arthur Miller*. Edinburgh and London: Oliver and Boyd, 1961.

Williams, Raymond, 'The Realism of Authur Miller' in *Critical Quarterly*. London: 1 (1959), pp 140 ff.

Odets, Clifford

Brenman-Gibson, Margaret, *Clifford Odets: American Playwright*. New York: Atheneum, 1982.

O'Neill, Eugene

Clark, Barrett H, *Eugene O'Neill: The Man and his Plays*. New York: Dover, 1947.

Gelb, Arthur and Barbara, *O'Neill*. New York: Harper and Row, 1962.

Rice, Elmer

Rice, Elmer, *The Living Theatre*. London: Heinemann, 1959.

Rice, Elmer, *Minority Reports: An autobiography*. London: Heinemann, 1963.

Riggs, Lynn

Riggs, Lynn, *The Cherokee Night and Other Plays*. Oklahoma: University of Oklahoma Press, 2003.

Simon, Neil

Garrison, Gary Wayne, 'An examination of the comedic techniques found in selected works of Neil Simon', unpublished thesis, North Texas State University, 1980.

Williams, Tennessee

Roudané, Matthew C, ed, *The Cambridge Companion to Tennessee Williams*. Cambridge: Cambridge University Press, 1997.

Spoto, Donald, *The Kindness of Strangers, the Life of Tennessee Williams*. New York: Ballantine Books, 1985.

Williams, Tennessee, *Memoirs*. Garden City: Doubleday, 1975.

Books about actors, designers and other theatre professionals

Harold Prince

Hirsch, Foster, *Harold Prince and the American Musical Theatre*. New York: Cambridge University Press, 1989.

Novelists: biography and criticism

Atherton, Gertrude

McClure, Charlotte S, *Atherton*, 1979.

Cather, Willa

Lee, Hermione, *Willa Cather: A Life Saved Up*, 1989.

Dreiser, Theodore

Dreiser, Theodore, *The Letters of Theodore Dreiser*, 1959.

Faulkner, William

Karl, Frederick R, *William Faulkner: American Writer*, 1989.

Hemingway, Ernest

Baker, Carlos, *Ernest Hemingway: A Life Story*, 1969.

James, Henry

Edel, Leon, *The Life of Henry James, 1953–72*.

Salinger, J D

Hamilton, Ian, *In Search of J D Salinger*, 1988.

Sinclair, Upton

Sinclair, Upton, *My Lifetime in Letters*, 1960.

Steinbeck, John

Steinbeck, John, *Steinbeck: A Life in Letters*, 1975.

Poetry anthologies

Ellman, Richard ed, *The New Oxford Book of American Verse*. New York: 1976.

Hall, Donald, ed, *American Poetry: An Introductory Anthology*. London: 1969.

Moore, Geoffrey, ed, *The Penguin Book of American Verse*. Harmondsworth: Penguin Books, 1977.

Vendler, Helen, *The Anthology of Contemporary American Poetry*. London: I B Tauris, 1986.

General works on contemporary American poetry

Hart, James D, ed, *The Oxford Companion to American Literature*. New York: 1975.

Jones, Peter, *Fifty American Poets*. London: Heinemann, 1980

Poets: biography and criticism

Frost, Robert

Brower, Reuben A, *Poetry of Robert Frost: Constellations of Intention*. New York: 1969.

Latham, Edward Connery, ed, *Interviews with Robert Frost*. London: 1967.

Poirier, Richard, *Robert Frost*. London: 1978.

Plath, Sylvia

Aird, Eileen, *The Art of Sylvia Plath*. Edinburgh: 1973.

Newman, Charles, ed, *The Art of Sylvia Plath*. London: 1970.

Pound, Ezra

Fraser, G S, *Ezra Pound*. Edinburgh: 1960.

Homberger, Eric, ed, *Ezra Pound*. London: 1972 (a collection of critical essays).

Stock, Noel, *A Life of Ezra Pound*. London: 1970.

Sullivan, J P, ed, *Ezra Pound*. Harmondsworth: Penguin Books, 1970.

4. POINTS FOR DISCUSSION

- Is it possible to transfer from one presentational medium to another without a loss of integrity? Use twentieth-century American dramas to illustrate your thesis.

- Account for the popularity of the tragedies of fifth century Greece amongst American playwrights.

- Do domestic circumstances offer sufficient interest to build a play on them? Use some American plays to illustrate your point of view.
- What part did Freud and Jung play in the development of the American drama?
- 'Poverty was a valuable theme in twentieth century American drama.' Discuss.
- Has loneliness a role to play in some American dramas?

5.   NOTES AND REFERENCES

1   Christopher Bigsby, 'A British View of an American Playwright' in Stephen R Centola, ed, *The Achievement of Arthur Miller: New Essays*. Dallas: Contemporary Research Associates, 1995.

2   Arthur Miller, *Collected Plays*. New York: Viking Press, 1957, 1. 19.

3   Arthur Miller, *The Crucible in History and Other Essays*. London: Methuen, 2000, p 71.

4   Matthew C. Roudané, ed, *Conversations with Arthur Miller*. Jackson: Jackson University Press of Mississippi, 1987, pp 179, 360.

5   Kenneth Tynan reviewing the London production of *A View from the Bridge*, *The Observer*, 14 October 1956.

6   *The Misfits*, p 5.

7   Arthur Miller, *Timebends: A Life*. New York: Grove Press, 1987.

8   Cited in Robert Jordan, *The Convict Theatres of Early Australia*, 1788–1840. Hatfield: University of Hertfordshire Press, 2002, p 54.

9   Entry on Henry James in *The Continuum Encyclopedia of British Literature*, eds Steven R Serafin and Valerie Grosvenor Myer. New York and London: Continuum, 2003.